Complete Guide to
PRIMARY
GYMNASTICS

Lindsay Broomfield
Gymnastics Consultant

Human Kinetics

Library of Congress Cataloging-in-Publication Data

Broomfield, Lindsay, 1968-
  Complete guide to primary gymnastics / Lindsay Broomfield.
    p. cm.
  Includes bibliographical references.
  ISBN-13: 978-0-7360-8658-5 (soft cover)
  ISBN-10: 0-7360-8658-7 (soft cover)
  1. Gymnastics. I. Title.
  GV461.B718 2011
  796.44--dc22

2010030722

ISBN-10: 0-7360-8658-7 (print)
ISBN-13: 978-0-7360-8658-5 (print)

The Web addresses cited in this text were current as of July 20, 2010, unless otherwise noted.

Acquisitions Editor: John Dickinson, PhD; **Developmental Editor:** Amy Stahl; **Assistant Editors:** Rachel Brito, Elizabeth Evans; **Copyeditor:** Jan Feeney; **Permission Manager:** Dalene Reeder; **Graphic Designer:** Fred Starbird; **Graphic Artist:** Denise Lowry; **Cover Designer:** Keith Blomberg; **DVD Face Designer:** Susan Rothermel Allen; **Photographer (cover and interior):** Neil Bernstein; **Photo Production Manager:** Jason Allen; **Art Manager:** Kelly Hendren; **Associate Art Manager and Illustrator:** Alan L. Wilborn; **Printer:** United Graphics

We thank Rising Stars Academy in Bloomington, Illinois, USA, for assistance in providing the location for the photo and video shoot for this book.

The contents of this DVD are licensed for private home use and traditional, face-to-face classroom instruction only. For public performance licensing, please contact a sales representative at **www.HumanKinetics.com/SalesRepresentatives.**

Printed in the United States of America   10 9 8 7 6 5 4 3 2 1

The paper in this book is certified under a sustainable forestry program.

Human Kinetics
Web site: www.HumanKinetics.com

Europe: Human Kinetics, 107 Bradford Road, Stanningley, Leeds LS28 6AT, United Kingdom
+44 (0) 113 255 5665
e-mail: hk@hkeurope.com

United States: Human Kinetics, P.O. Box 5076, Champaign, IL 61825-5076
800-747-4457
e-mail: humank@hkusa.com

Canada: Human Kinetics, 475 Devonshire Road Unit 100, Windsor, ON N8Y 2L5
800-465-7301 (in Canada only)
e-mail: info@hkcanada.com

Australia: Human Kinetics, 57A Price Avenue, Lower Mitcham, South Australia 5062
08 8372 0999
e-mail: info@hkaustralia.com

New Zealand: Human Kinetics, P.O. Box 80, Torrens Park, South Australia 5062
0800 222 062
e-mail: info@hknewzealand.com

E4933

Contents

Preface   vii

Acknowledgments   x

How to Use This Book and DVD Package   xi

DVD Contents   xix

PART 1 Teaching Primary School Gymnastics · · · · · · · · · 1

CHAPTER 1 Developing Fundamental Movement Skills Through Gymnastics · · · · · · · · · · 3

What Are Fundamental Movement Skills?   3

Physical Development Patterns in Children   4

Body Management Skills   5

Locomotor Skills   11

Object Control Skills   13

Physical Literacy Skills   14

CHAPTER 2 Ensuring Effective Delivery of Gymnastics in Primary Education · · · · 17

Planning for Gymnastics in Primary Education   17

Learning In and Through Gymnastics   18

Implementing the Foundation Stage:
   Early Learning Goals for Physical Education   18

Implementing the National Curriculum: Four Key Aspects
   of Learning in Key Stage 1 and Key Stage 2   19

Linking Information and Communication Technology
   With Gymnastics   23

Inclusion and Differentiation Objectives   24

Class Management and Organisation   24

CHAPTER **3** **Using Apparatus in Primary Gymnastics** · · · · · · · · · · · **29**

Using Large Apparatus   29
Using Hand Apparatus   32
Impermissible Apparatus for Primary Schools   38

CHAPTER **4** **Attainment and Assessment** · · · · · · · · **39**

Foundation Stage Profile for Assessment   39
Key Stage 1 and Key Stage 2 Physical Education
    Attainment Targets: Level Descriptions 1 to 5   40
Guidelines for Assessing Gymnastics
    Performances in Key Stage 1 and Key Stage 2   40
Features of Progressions in Gymnastics
    Based on the Scheme of Work on the DVD   42

PART **II** **Gymnastics Warm-Up, Cool-Down, Techniques and Games** · · **45**

CHAPTER **5** **Preparing For and Recovering From Physical Activity** · · · · · · · · · · · **47**

Preparing for Physical Activity: The Warm-Up   47
Recovering from Physical Activity: The Cool-Down   56

CHAPTER **6** **Basic Gymnastics Shapes** · · · · · · · · · · **59**

Stretch Shape   59
Tuck Shape   61
Star Shape   62
Straddle Shape   64
Pike Shape   65

CHAPTER **7** **Postural Shapes** · · · · · · · · · · · · **69**

Box Shape   69
Front Support   70

Back Support   70
Arch Shape   71
Dish Shape   72

CHAPTER **8** Rolling Techniques · · · · · · · · · · · **75**

Stretch Roll   75
Tuck Roll   77
Side Roll   78
Half Roll   79
Straddle Roll   80
Forward Roll   82

CHAPTER **9** Inversions · · · · · · · · · · · · · **85**

Bridge   85
Handstand   86
Cartwheel   90

CHAPTER **10** Partner Work · · · · · · · · · · · **95**

Base and Top: Who Is Who?   95
Scheme of Work   95
Top Postural Shapes   96
Box Base Balances   97
Counterbalance and Countertension   99

CHAPTER **11** Themed Games · · · · · · · · · · **103**

Space Finding Numbers   103
Gymnastics Beans   106
Road Traffic Signs   108
Washing the Clothes   112
Creature Movements   114
Physical Literacy Ideas   119

Bibliography   121
About the Author   123
DVD User Instructions   124

Preface

During my time working with primary teachers, several concerns and needs have surfaced regarding the teaching of gymnastics in primary education. *Complete Guide to Primary Gymnastics* provides answers to those issues. This book and DVD package is a teaching resource that will inspire you to instruct and meet the requirements of the gymnastics syllabus as defined by the foundation stage early learning goals and the primary National Curriculum.

Gymnastics is a key activity in physical education and understanding of physical development, health and well-being. Instruction in gymnastics will ensure that all pupils have the opportunity to develop and acquire basic physical skills. Fundamental movement skills are movement patterns, the precursors to physical skill acquisition. Gymnastics-like activities promote the development of fundamental movement skills and physical literacy. In the context of this teaching resource, physical literacy refers to the ability to interpret and instruct the body to perform an action accurately and with confidence and to recognize the physical, social, cognitive and emotional attributes required to do so. Children's competence in physical literacy encourages creativity and confidence during all physical movement activities. Therefore if a pupil can demonstrate competence in the fundamental skill categories of body management, locomotor skills and object control skills, then that pupil can be deemed to be physically literate. The pupil is able to move freely, demonstrating confident total-body management, expression and leadership skills. Development of physical literacy also allows children to move in a safe and effective manner. Gymnastics is frequently recognised as a good foundation sport through which all fundamental movement skills can be learnt.

Complete Guide to Primary Gymnastics consists of a book and a bound-in DVD. The book begins by explaining how physical development patterns influence the learning of basic physical skills. It then covers the step-by-step instruction of gymnastics skill acquisition. The DVD contains a unique set of pictorial resources and short video clips that complement the book and will prove invaluable to experienced and inexperienced teachers and all pupils.

The gymnastics scheme of work included on the DVD plots the progression of gymnastics skill development through the seven years of primary education (year R through year 6). The units of work all link to the foundation stage early learning goals and the primary National Curriculum guidelines. Gymnastics is commonly perceived as a specialist sport that involves high-risk activities, but this teaching resource allays those misconceptions and proves that gymnastics is attainable to all and straightforward to teach. If you are a primary teacher with little knowledge or experience in teaching gymnastics activities, you will find the step-by-step instructions invaluable. If you are a more experienced and confident teacher, you will find the ideas and themes in the units of work to be exciting and challenging ways of improving pupils' learning.

This resource promotes the adaptability of gymnastics through its cross-curricular links, thus complementing the cross-curricular studies strand of learning in the primary curriculum, where it is important to recognise that some pupils prefer or are able to demonstrate their understanding of other areas of learning more effectively through movement than through classroom-based activities such as writing, drawing and talking. Another unique feature is the recognition of the role computers play in today's society with each unit of work including an ICT (information, communication and technology) task. *Complete Guide to Primary Gymnastics* thus promotes the notion of learning in and through gymnastics. Teachers in primary schools can expect to do the following:

- Promote physical skill acquisition
- Enable pupils to learn about and respect their bodies
- Encourage individual cognitive development
- Encourage social development and cooperation (working in partners and in small groups)
- Enhance self-confidence and self-esteem
- Enhance physical skill learning through cross-curricular studies and ICT

Complete Guide to Primary Gymnastics is based on teaching and learning gymnastics through a unique and simple gymnastics formula. First pupils learn five basic gymnastics shapes (stretch, tuck, star, straddle and pike); then by applying an action from the fundamental skill categories (balance, jump, invert, roll, travel), they can learn a gymnastics-specific skill.

shape + action = gymnastics skill

Empowering pupils with knowledge of gymnastics shapes and actions will enable them to move and respond safely during their gymnastics lessons. Pupils are taught to describe and verbalise their shapes and actions, thus enhancing their understanding of the body movements that they and others are creating. This encourages the correct use of vocabulary and standardises learning in the gymnastics environment.

Through my current employment as a primary school gymnastics consultant and tutor, I have had the opportunity to work alongside many primary teachers and to listen to their concerns regarding the user-friendliness of existing gymnastics resources and schemes of work. Of primary concern was that existing schemes did not relate directly to the current primary National Curriculum guidelines or meet the early learning goals of the foundation stage. In *Complete Guide to Primary Gymnastics*, every unit of work and progression relates to the early learning goals in the foundation stage and the primary National Curriculum guidelines in key stage 1 and key stage 2.

Teachers also have expressed their concern that existing schemes allow for very little progressive development. Their complaints are that they seem to be teaching the same objectives and expecting the same outcomes in gymnastics in year 5 as they did in year 2. The scheme of work in *Complete Guide to Primary Gymnastics* is progressive, based on development from the basics. The main focus of the foundation stage is the establishment of elementary movement skills through simple physical coordination activities. In particular, children learn the fundamentals of body management, locomotor skills and object control skills based on basic gymnastics activities. At key stage 1 the focus continues in developing fundamental movement skills, but it introduces more gymnastics-specific skills. At key stage 2 the previously learnt skills become channelled into themed units of work.

Many teachers also think that existing resources offered poor, if any, guidance regarding the basics of gymnastics, such as the gymnastics shapes and skills and how to teach them. *Complete Guide to Primary Gymnastics*, through its pictorial resources and short video clips on the DVD, shows the basics and how to build on them, making it an invaluable aid to those teachers with an interest in developing gymnastics activities.

In other gymnastics resources, there is scant use of gymnastics vocabulary, which is vital to the correct teaching and learning of gymnastics. The correct gymnastics vocabulary is highlighted on each of the Pictorial Resource cards on the DVD with the use of thought bubbles.

Currently the enormous gap between what is expected of pupils in a year 6 primary school gymnastics lesson and what is expected of them in a year 7 secondary school lesson is not accommodated by other resources; that is, those resources fail to prepare children for the transition. The scheme of work in *Complete Guide to Primary Gymnastics*—with its progressive approach of building on the basics, establishing partner and group work and using correct gymnastics vocabulary—enables pupils to be physically and psychologically competent as they enter secondary school armed with a better understanding of gymnastics-specific skills.

Critics tend to view gymnastics as a very isolated, individual activity, allowing little opportunity for children to practise social and peer group interaction. My response in this resource has been to introduce partner work in the form of paired balances and other activities that encourage children to work in small groups, allowing for social interaction, leadership and communication skills to develop.

This resource contains a whole chapter on using apparatus (chapter 3). In general, there is very little understanding of uses for large apparatus in school gym halls; many children are not given the opportunity to use wall bars and similar equipment other than in their early years. In many schools, large apparatus is underused or misused often as a display unit or a storage facility. *Complete Guide to Primary Gymnastics* emphasises the use of large apparatus by all the year groups, offering specific guidance about which skills and exercises can be learnt and developed at each stage of instruction. These skills and exercises are supported by illustrations regarding apparatus layouts, pictorial resources and video clips on the DVD. This resource is also unique in its inclusion of hand apparatus in a gymnastics environment. The activities enable pupils to develop their creative skills and promote the learning of object control skills.

In many other gymnastics resources, there is ambiguity surrounding safety guidelines, such as when to use or not to use mats. This resource offers guidance on safe practice that can be read in conjunction with, but not as a substitute for, each education authority's and individual school's policy on such issues. I direct all readers to the Association for Physical Education,

Safe Practice in Physical Education and School Sport (2008), by Peter Whitlam and Glen Beaumont, but the official literature of public bodies remains the primary authority on creating a safe environment for children. This resource draws awareness to the particular ways of teaching gymnastics safely. Chapter 1 of *Complete Guide to Primary Gymnastics* also highlights the physical development patterns in young children, recognising the limitations in physical skill acquisition that these patterns of development can cause. This resource offers ideas and examples throughout, providing simple formulas that can evolve or be adapted and novel variations of standard movements and exercises.

Gymnastics is an ideal foundation sport that comprehensively introduces fundamental movement skills that enable young athletes to move into any chosen sport at a later date. Teaching basic gymnastics enables participants to feel how their bodies work and to become responsible for their movements. Gymnastics trains the pathways of communication between the brain and the body and in its simplest form ensures that all movement is carried out in a controlled, safe manner. Gymnastics is also good fun and self-rewarding.

Acknowledgments

I owe my gratitude to the primary teachers in the Trafalger cluster of primary schools in Salisbury, Wiltshire (St. Edmunds School Sports Partnership), who provided me with the inspiration and motivation to write this teaching resource. I am also grateful to Pam Swienton, a colleague and friend, for supporting its inclusion and for giving her time freely when I have been in need of advice. These primary teachers have trialled, challenged and questioned all the teaching techniques, ideas, games and themes to such an extent that I, too, have indeed been trialled and challenged! I am continually rewarded by the very successful and entertaining gymnastics festivals held annually by the Trafalger cluster teachers and pupils as a direct result of using the teaching resource in their gymnastics lessons. Their enthusiasm and high quality of gymnastics give me every confidence that this teaching resource will prove a source of joy and encouragement to all teachers and pupils alike.

How to Use This Book and DVD Package

Complete Guide to Primary Gymnastics is presented in two complementary formats: a book and a DVD enabling you to review and instruct through a visually stimulating process and enabling pupils to learn through observation. The teaching resource is easy to navigate; the instruction is based on a simple gymnastics formula:

shape + action = gymnastics skills

The book explains the notion of learning in and through gymnastics and guides you through delivery strategies before demonstrating through step-by-step progressions how to instruct basic gymnastics skills.

How to Use the DVD

Icons are placed throughout the book to indicate when further information is available on the DVD. The DVD icon appears at right. When you insert the DVD into your computer, you will be presented with four folders:

1. Book Photos
2. Dartfish Mediabooks
3. Pictorial Resources
4. Scheme of Work

In each of the four main folders are sub-folders that contain specific files. These are listed in the DVD contents on page xix. All the files in the scheme of work and pictorial resources are labelled and can be readily printed for personal use or to share with your pupils. The video clips are also readily accessible for you to share with your pupils as needed. In addition to the pictorial resources, all of the photos from the book are included on the DVD along with a blank Power-Point template, which allows you to create your own presentations using the book photos.

The scheme of work on the DVD plots the progress of gymnastics skill development through the seven years of primary education. It is divided into three sections:

- Foundation stage
- Key stage 1 (KS1)
- Key stage 2 (KS2)

In each key stage and each year group are gymnastics-specific units of work (16 total). Each unit of work focuses on developing fundamental movement skills through gymnastics activities, thus ensuring this teaching resource is specific to the sport of gymnastics. In the foundation stage and key stage 1, all the elements of gymnastics are introduced, repeated and rehearsed, providing pupils with the skills and knowledge to tackle the themed ideas in key stage 2.

The DVD contains a unique collection of pictorial resources that visually take you and your pupils through simple progressions to acquiring gymnastics skills. In addition, a compilation of video clips will aid in visual representation of complete gymnastics skills and sequences of gymnastics skills, therefore enhancing learning. All the gymnastics skills, themed ideas (key stage 2 units) and themed games (warm-up activities) are supported in the extensive set of pictorial resources. In addition to being educational and informative, these images are a colourful and eye-catching feature to the resource. Visual stimulation is a powerful instrument, and the pictorial resources provide an easily accessible visual learning tool. All pupils, however young, are very adept at copying. The pictorial resources have the following features:

- Colourful pictures
- Technical advice
- Guidance on health and safety concerns
- Progressive steps
- Thought bubbles using correct vocabulary

Scheme of Work

Each unit of work offers an overview of the featured gymnastics activities, with focused learning intentions and learning outcomes and links to the relevant early learning goals and primary National Curriculum guidelines. The unit of work then presents a list of progressions similar to that of a lesson plan and guidelines to organising the apparatus in a colourful apparatus layout at the end of the unit.

The progressions should not be taken as individual lesson plans. Depending on each individual class and each individual teacher, it may be possible to teach more than one progression in a single lesson, or it may be necessary to stay at a progression for several weeks to ensure that pupils understand all the tasks and accomplish them safely.

The progressions can be implemented in a prescriptive manner or used just to extract ideas, which are then put into practice to suit the individual needs of the class. It is not a requirement to complete all the progressions in each unit of work as each progression has its own learning intentions and learning outcomes. Visual resources accompany most units of work on the DVD to aid visual learning and are a useful addition if you are unable to present a live demonstration. The 16 units of work on the DVD are outlined as follows.

Foundation Stage

Pupils should attempt all the units of work in the foundation stage. Finding a space, making basic shapes, balancing, jumping and landing and rolling introduce the prerequisite skills for the further use in the scheme of work. It is not necessary to complete all the progressions in each unit of work, but to maximise a pupil's learning potential and understanding of basic safety requirements and fundamental movement skills, all pupils should attempt at least the early progressions from each unit.

Unit 1: Space, Listening Pose, Movement Patterns and Basic Shapes

This first unit of work develops and reinforces the concept of space through the use of the Space Finding Numbers game and introduces the listening pose, a requirement for discipline and control. Through the use of the Gymnastics Beans game, pupils are introduced to the concept of shapes and actions, which form the basis of the gymnastics formula. The game is also a fun way to discuss and explore ways of moving and travelling, using the various parts of the body and developing an understanding and awareness of personal and general space. This unit provides pupils with the opportunity to use large apparatus and hand apparatus.

Unit 2: Basic Shapes and Balances: Stretch Shape, Tuck Shape and Star Shape

This unit of work continues to explore three of the five basic gymnastics shapes: the stretch, the tuck and the star shape. It provides pupils with the knowledge and vocabulary of these shapes and an understanding of the action of balance to promote body management and control. This unit

of work provides pupils with the opportunity to use large apparatus and hand apparatus.

Unit 3: Encouraging Safe Dismounts

This action-packed unit of work introduces the essential concept of the action jump and land. Children physically develop in a cephalocaudal manner, which means gaining control of the body in a head-to-foot order. As a result, children gain control (that is, strength and awareness) of the lower limbs after they gain control of the upper body, a fact addressed in this unit by focusing on the actions of jumping and travelling. The three basic gymnastics shapes (stretch, tuck and star) are implemented into jumps and employed to vary travelling skills. Pupils explore various ways to travel along ropes on the floor, benches and wall bars. The skill of skipping is an integral component of this unit and beneficial for young pupils to learn; it develops physical fitness and coordination whilst promoting physiological benefits and social interaction. This unit also enables pupils to learn the correct transport and handling of large apparatus.

Unit 4: Early Rolling Techniques and Climbing

This unit of work focuses on applying the basic gymnastics shapes to the actions of rolling and climbing, thus introducing pupils to the gymnastics formula for developing gymnastics-specific skills. Both these actions are early movement patterns performed naturally by most infants. The stretch roll and tuck roll are performed on the mats; the stretch, star and tuck shapes are performed on the wall bars. The Road Traffic Signs game continues to promote basic gymnastics shapes and adds a fun dimension to the warm up. This unit continues to encourage pupils to correctly transport and handle large apparatus.

Key Stage 1

In key stage 1, pupils should complete at least one unit of work involving balance skills, rolling skills and jump, land and travel skills to maximise their learning and understanding of basic safety requirements and fundamental movement skills.

Unit 5: Balances on Large and Small Body Parts Alongside Skipping

Year 1: Balance is a fundamental skill with its integral components of body management and body control. The activity of skipping has many progressions and variations that promote physiological, emotional and social development. This unit of work encourages pupils to develop the fundamental movement skills of body management through balance and body awareness activities and object control skills through skipping activities with a rope. The cool-down section of the lesson promotes the development of core stability through postural shapes that will aid balance skills. Pupils also have the opportunity to transfer learnt skills to the large apparatus.

Year 2: Pupils progress the skipping activity with a skipping rope to explore low-impact and high-impact activities. Pupils continue to select and apply learnt balance skills on large and small body parts and begin to compose short sequences with a focus on presentation and use of arms, head, legs and feet. Pupils also have the opportunity to transfer learnt skills to the large apparatus.

Unit 6: Basic Shapes, Additional Rolling Techniques and Climbing

Year 1: This unit of work combines knowledge of the five basic gymnastics shapes with the actions of rolling and climbing. It may be necessary for pupils to revisit the stretch shape, star shape and tuck shape before you introduce the pike shape and straddle shape in the Washing the Clothes game in the warm up. The five shapes form the basis of most of the gymnastics skills covered in the scheme of work. Pupils' understanding of these properties will form a foundation from which actions can be applied, resulting in sport-specific skill acquisition through the gymnastics formula. Most pupils with a sound knowledge of the shapes and an understanding of the rolling technique will be able to attempt the rolls safely and effectively. Large apparatus, such as the wall bars, generate a fun atmosphere where most pupils attempt climbing skills that promote the development of upper-body strength.

Year 2: Pupils continue to build on their knowledge of the basic gymnastics shapes and rolling techniques to apply them in the composition of short sequences. By the end of the unit in year 2, most pupils should be able to demonstrate physically and describe verbally the basic gymnastics shapes and their associated properties. Pupils experiment with performing the basic gymnastics shapes on large and small body parts (introduced in unit 5). Pupils perform basic gymnastics shapes on, under or over large apparatus with a focus on developing linking skills to introduce and solidify the concept of composing sequences. The hoop is used in the cool-down, allowing pupils to experiment with movement patterns.

Unit 7: Jump, Land and Travel

Year 1: This unit focuses on learning various modes of travel through the themed game Crea-

ture Movements, which is an imaginative pictorial display emphasising movement patterns of animals. The importance of the spot landing is revisited and reinforced through simple progressions. Learnt skills are transferred to the large apparatus, and movement patterns with a ribbon are explored during the hand apparatus activity.

Year 2: Travelling and movement patterns are extended to include a change of direction: spinning and turning. Shapes are also implemented into jumps, and the importance of the spot landing is reinforced. Creature Movement resources continue to be a good source of fun; in this year group, pupils use the movement patterns to compose short sequences. Learnt skills are transferred to the large apparatus.

Many activities included in both the year 1 and year 2 jump, land and travel units focus on promoting the awareness of lower-limb movements to develop control and strength.

Key Stage 2

In key stage 2, both units in each year group should be attempted. It is not necessary to complete all the progressions in each unit.

Unit 8: Mix 'n' Mingle Balances

This is a fun unit of work that can be used in any of the key stage 2 year groups. Mix 'n' Mingle involves balances on large and small body parts and requires pupils to work in teams to solve physical literacy challenges. The ideas in this unit have proven to be attainable yet challenging to most pupils and have a massive scope for creativity. It is easy to instruct the Mix 'n' Mingle activities; they can also be carried out safely in restricted areas and can be organised quickly when time is limited. The use of hand apparatus can add further diversity and scope to the activities. This unit of work provides an opportunity to explore sequencing and to advance evaluating and improving techniques among your pupils.

Year 3

In year 3, pupils are encouraged to work with a partner. In unit 9, pupils work together in pairs or in small groups working with the basic gymnastics shapes to develop creative ideas. In unit 10, simple paired balances are introduced, which encourage pupils to share responsibility for achieving gymnastics-specific skills.

Unit 9: Symmetry and Group Balances

This unit is cross-curricular and links with symmetry projects from the mathematics curriculum. The unit of work focuses on the properties and technical points of the five basic gymnastics shapes (stretch, star, tuck, straddle and pike) and explores ways to demonstrate the shapes in various formations to perform balances in partners and small groups. The rules governing the acquisition of symmetrical and asymmetrical shapes provide problem-solving challenges to your pupils, and creating group balances will challenge pupils to work together as a team. Hand apparatus (ribbons, chiffons and any other flowing material) are implemented, encouraging pupils to focus their feelings and emotions on physical movement patterns.

Unit 10: Partner Up and Roll

This unit introduces partner work, where cooperation with and responsibility to others are the prime focus. Before commencing this unit, you should be familiar with the guidelines on working with a partner. (See chapter 10 in this book.) Pupils are introduced to specific vocabulary regarding the roles of the bases and tops in paired balances that require pupils to support the partial weight of their partner. Building on their knowledge of basic gymnastics shapes (stretch, star, tuck, straddle and pike) and postural shapes (box, front support and back support), this unit of work allows pupils choice and the opportunity to develop ideas in a compositional manner. Pupils revisit rolling techniques from unit 6 (Basic Shapes, Additional Rolling Techniques and Climbing) and select and apply learnt skills to compose short sequences with their partners.

Year 4

In year 4, pupils are presented with two contrasting units of work. The first unit explores the development of locomotor skills and travelling techniques. Unit 12 focuses on the action of balance in the form of paired balances and the use of the basic gymnastics shapes where pupils are encouraged to use their observation and verbalisation skills.

Unit 11: Flighted Foot Patterns

The body can elevate itself from the ground in many forms, take on a variety of shapes and travel using varied movement patterns. This unit of work revolves around four combinations of foot patterns that can project the body from the floor into flight: jump, hop, leap and hurdle skills. Continuing with resources from the themed game Creature Movements, pupils explore ways to travel, compose short sequences and incorporate hand apparatus. Short sequences are also composed by pupils with the use of flighted foot patterns and ropes on the floor. Pupils use the large apparatus with an introduction to simple vaulting techniques.

Unit 12: Building Boxes and Bridges

This unit focuses on the acquisition of balance. Working with partners, pupils perform box base balances and build bridge-like constructions. When pupils have acquired a repertoire of box base balance skills, they are encouraged to compose short sequences. Following the bridge theme, pupils work with a partner using the five basic gymnastics shapes to perform a shape over a shape, which they are asked to verbally describe (such as a straddle on hands and feet over a stretch on back). Pupils then transfer their bridge-like constructions to the large apparatus. Pupils also have the opportunity to learn a gymnastics-specific inversion skill, the bridge. Hand apparatus in the form of balls are introduced, and pupils explore moving the ball around, under and over the body to enhance stretching exercises.

Year 5

In year 5, the focus in the first unit is towards developing compositional sequences using different themes. In unit 14, pupils further develop their paired balances promoting their knowledge of simple biomechanics before implementing the learnt skills into sequences using the large apparatus.

Unit 13: Mirror, Match and Canon

This unit encourages teamwork in small groups. Through cross-curricular links to music, it promotes acquisition of rhythm and timing to ensure that short sequences are performed effectively. This unit of work involves linking previously learnt actions such as rolling, balancing, travelling, and jumping and landing into non-contact short sequences done in a mirror image (side by side), in a matching fashion (moving away and moving together) or in a canon action (leading and following). This is a fun unit of work where pupils learn to value the contributions from all members of a partnership or small group. Hand apparatus and large apparatus can be introduced to the sequences.

Unit 14: Push, Pull and Skip

This unit of work requires pupils to understand the importance of centre of mass. They explore where the centre of mass lies (inside or outside the body depending on the skill they perform) and the role it plays in acquiring stability in partner work. Counterbalance (pushing) and countertension (pulling) skills are fun challenges that require trust and communication between the partners. The pushing counterbalances are the easiest, and the pulling countertensions are more challenging. When pupils have mastered a repertoire of counterbalance and countertension skills, they can transfer the skills to the large apparatus. Skipping activities promote the benefits of aerobic activity and encourage pupils to set goals and personal challenges. This unit also explores cross-curricular learning by encouraging pupils to use data collection techniques in numeracy.

Year 6

In year 6, pupils are given the opportunity to review the skills that they have learnt and implement them into compositional sequences using a change mechanism to alter the overall appearance. The last unit in the scheme of work provides pupils with the opportunity to develop their gymnastics-specific skills based on the theme of rotation around an axis.

Unit 15: All Change

Pupils are introduced to simple change mechanisms, which alter the appearance of an action or sequence of actions (rolling, jump and land, balance and travelling) when performed in a short compositional sequence. The change mechanisms involve altering the direction of movement, the tempo of movement or the level of movement. Pupils transfer short sequences to the large apparatus. The themed game Creature Movements assists pupils in understanding the application of a change mechanism to learnt movement patterns.

Unit 16: Rock, Roll and Invert

This is the most skill-focused gymnastics unit that covers rolling techniques, jumping and turning skills, and inversions (handstands and cartwheels) to demonstrate the movements that occur around each axis of rotation: vertical (longitudinal), horizontal, and lateral. Hand apparatus are also implemented so that pupils can demonstrate movement around each of the rotational axes.

Resource Examples From the DVD

In the scheme of work, each unit of work provides an overview of the gymnastics content and how the skills are developed through the four key aspects of learning. Each progression has a learning objective which is explained in the form of learning intentions and learning outcomes. All units of work provide cross-curricular links. The unit then lists the progressions that are arranged to show the early learning goal or national curriculum learning intention, the activities included in this progression with teaching points and references to pictorial resources or video clips, which are available on the DVD. The activity section and corresponding literature is divided into three sections, the pre-activity which focuses on the preparation or warm up period, the main activity which focuses on the core tasks of the lesson followed by the post activity which focuses on the recovery or cool down period. The pictorial resources provide a visual representation of skills for pupils and teaching aids for teachers with a directive to using the correct vocabulary. Required equipment is listed and at the end of some units of work there is an example of how to set up the large apparatus and hand apparatus.

 Refer to the DVD for the scheme of work.

On the top of page xvi is an example of the four key aspects of learning, learning objectives, and cross-curricular links outline:

Unit 6 (1) Basic Shapes, Additional Rolling Techniques and Climbing

Following are the four key aspects of learning (aspects closely interlink) KS1:

From Qualification and Curriculum Development Agency. Available: http://curriculum.qcda.gov.uk/key-stages-1-and-2/subjects/physical-education/keystage2/index.aspx

Acquiring and Developing Skills

Learn the basic skills of the straddle shape and tuck shape on different parts of the body and understand the concept of rolling and changing direction. Repeat and rehearse five basic gymnastics shapes.

Selecting and Applying Skill, Tactics and Compositional Ideas

Select the learnt skills of the straddle shape and tuck shape and apply them into a rolling activity learning the straddle roll and half tuck roll skills, focusing on the importance of start and finish positions. Select basic gymnastics shapes to transfer to the large apparatus.

Evaluating and Improving

Consider technical points and properties of the basic gymnastics shapes with a focus towards improving presentation skills to evaluate both one's own and others' performances.

Knowledge and Understanding of Fitness and Health

Understand the safety requirements of using mats to perform rolling skills, and the body awareness required to maintain the straddle shape and tuck shape and those benefits associated with undertaking the rolling skills safely in a controlled manner.

The following key aspect of knowledge and understanding of fitness and health should be discussed freely throughout the lesson or before and after when either preparing pupils for the activity or recapping events after the lesson:

- How important it is to be active

Learning Intentions and Learning Outcomes

Progression 1 learning intention: Introduce all of the basic gymnastics shapes and postural shapes.

From L. Broomfield, 2011, *Complete Guide to Primary Gymnastics* (Champaign, IL: Human Kinetics).

Following is an example of a lesson progression outline:

Learning intention of national curriculum	Year 1 Basic Shapes, Additional Rolling Techniques and Climbing progression 4			Resources
	Activity	Equipment	Teaching points	
	Find a space and adopt listening pose.	Non-slip markers	Identify properties of a space.	
1a 1b 3a	Warm-up pulse raiser: Washing the Clothes game. Repeat concepts and associated basic and postural gymnastics shapes.		Ask pupils the following questions: • How many different shapes have you performed in the warm up game? (8 in total = 5 basic shapes + 3 postural shapes) • Can you correctly name the basic and postural gymnastics shapes?	Washing the Clothes game
4b	Mobility of the joints		Ask pupils to put their hand on the biceps muscle at the top of the arm. Feel the muscle contracting and relaxing as the hand moves towards and away from the shoulder. Explain that muscles are responsible for moving the body.	Mobility of joints
2a 2b	Activity stations x3 *Rolling activity 1 Choose from • a straddle roll, • a tuck roll or • a half roll and compose a short sequence.	Mats: discuss importance of safe transport of mats (H&S).	Ask pupils to do the following: • Show start and finish positions. • Implement a travelling movement pattern before and after the roll.	Tuck roll Half roll Straddle roll
1a 1b	*Hoop activity 1 • Hula-hooping	Hoops	Teach pupils to spin hoop and wiggle hips: very difficult to coordinate	Hoop activities
2b 2c	*Climbing activity 1 • Explore ways to perform the five basic shapes on the wall bars. • Can you link 2 shapes together?	Wall bars: discuss importance of climbing up and down and the use of no mats (H&S).	H&S instruct pupils to climb up and climb down from the wall bars. Teach pupils to perform a shape on the wall bars, descend, travel on the floor and perform a different shape on the wall bars.	Basic shape ideas for wall bars
3b 3c	Cool-down: shapes • Compose a short sequence using 3 of the basic gymnastics shapes. • Ask a partner to observe your routine and repeat it.	Hoops	With pupils discuss the importance of good body posture.	Basic shapes

From L. Broomfield, 2011, *Complete Guide to Primary Gymnastics* (Champaign, IL: Human Kinetics).

Following is an example of a Pictorial Resource card:

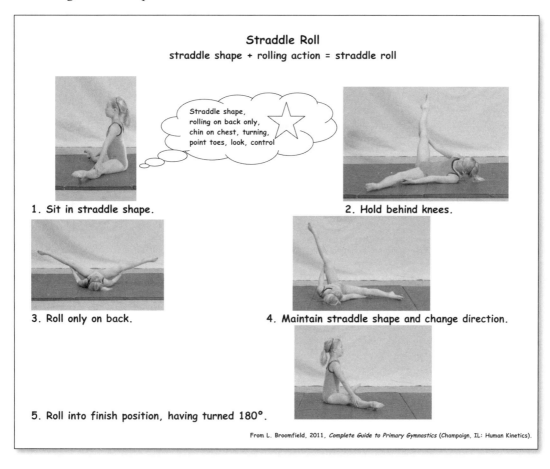

Following is an example of a suggested apparatus layout that you will find at the end of some units of work:

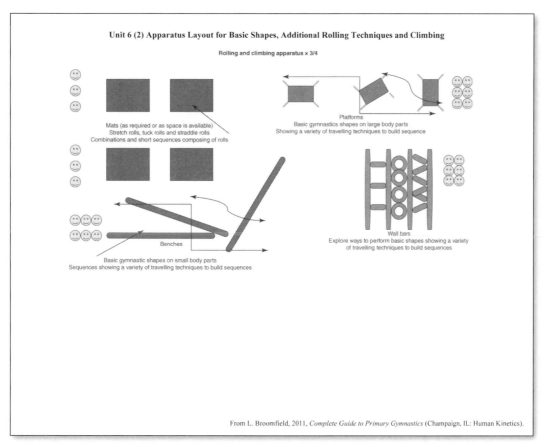

DVD Contents

Book Photos

Chapter 1
Chapter 2
Chapter 3
Chapter 5
Chapter 6
Chapter 7
Chapter 8
Chapter 9
Chapter 10
Chapter 11

Dartfish Mediabooks

Flighted Foot Patterns
  Jump
  Hop
  Leap
  Hurdle
  Linking flighted foot patterns
Inversions
  Sideways bunny jump: two feet
  Sideways bunny jump: one foot
  Bent-leg cartwheel
  Cartwheel
  Tucked bunny jump
  Handstand entrance and exit
  Half handstand
  Half handstand tapping feet
  Handstand
Rolling Techniques
  Stretch roll
  Tuck roll
  Side roll
  Straddle roll
  Half roll
  Learning the forward roll
  Forward roll
  Implementing shapes into stretch roll
  Implementing shapes into tuck roll
  Half roll Straddle roll
  Half roll Tuck roll
Warming Up
  Dynamic Stretching
    Heel raises
    Rotator
    Twister
    Buttock kicker
    Goose walk
    Coffee grinder

Mobility of the Joints
  Nodding
  Turning head
  Shrugging
  Backward shoulder rotation
  Backward arm rotation
  Forward arm rotation
  Alternate arm rotation
  Hand movements
  Arm movements
  Hip rotation
  Knee up
  Foot up to hand
  Heel and toe taps

Pictorial Resources

Balance Combinations
  Balance_Large_Body_Parts
  Balance_Small_Body_Parts
  Basic_Shapes_Group_Balances
  Mix_N_Mingle_Balances
  Shape_Ideas_For_Wall_Bars
  Symmetrical_Asymmetrical
Basic Biomechanics
  Rotation
  Rotation_Around_An_Axis
  Stability_And_Balance
  Wheres_My_Centre_Of_Mass
Basic Shapes
  Pike_Shape
  Star_Shape
  Straddle_Shape
  Stretch_Shape
  Tuck_Shape
Flight and Travel
  Change_Mechanisms
  Flighted_Foot_Patterns
  Spot_Landing
  Travel_Techniques
Inversions
  Bridge
  Cartwheel_Progressions
  Handstand_Progressions
Partner Work
  Box_Base_Balances
  Counterbalance_Pushing
  Countertension_Pulling
  Top_Postural_Shapes
Postural Shapes
  Arch_And_Dish

Box_Front_Back_Supports
Rolling Techniques
  Forward_Roll
  Half_Roll
  Learning_The_Forward_Roll
  Side_Roll
  Straddle_Roll
  Stretch_Roll
  Tuck_Roll
Themed Games
  Creature Movements
    Bouncing_Bunny
    Crawling_Caterpillar
    Creeping_Crocodile
    Fluttering_Butterfly
    Flying_Bird
    Galloping_Horse
    Jumping_Frog
    Lumbering_Bear
    Running_Spider
    Scampering_Monkey
    Scurrying_Crab
    Sliding_Snake
    Stomping_Elephant
    Swimming_Dolphin
  Gymnastics Beans
    Action_Frozen_Bean
    Action_Jelly_Bean
    Action_Jumping_Bean
    Action_Runner_Bean
    Shape_Baked_Bean
    Shape_Broad_Bean
    Shape_String_Bean
  Road Traffic Signs
    Action_Amber_Light
    Action_Green_Light
    Action_Red_Light
    Action_Roundabout
    Action_Speedbumps
    Shape_Overtaking
    Shape_Pedestrian_Crossing
    Shape_Road_Block
    Shape_Traffic_Jam
    Shape_Wide_Load
  Space Finding Numbers
    1_Super_Hero

    2_Jumping_Girls
    3_Winning_Boys
    4_Smiling_Girls
  Washing the Clothes
    Basic_Shape_Dress
    Basic_Shape_Shorts
    Basic_Shape_T_Shirt
    Basic_Shape_Trousers
    Basic_Shape_Washing_Line
    Postural_Shape_Clothes_Peg
    PosturalShp_IroningBoard
    PosturalShp_WashingMachine
    Washing_The_Clothes_Story
Using Hand Apparatus
  Balls
  Beanbags
  Hoops
  Ribbons
  Skipping_Ropes
Static Stretches

Scheme of Work

01_Contents
02_SchemeOfWorkGuidelines
03_PlanningForGymnastics
04_EarlyLearningGoals
05_Unit 1
06_Unit 2
07_Unit 3
08_Unit 4
09_KS1andKS2Gymnastics
10_Unit 5
11_Unit 6
12_Unit 7
13_Unit 8
14_Unit 9
15_Unit 10
16_Unit 11
17_Unit 12
18_Unit 13
19_Unit 14
20_Unit 15
21_Unit 16
22_ICT_With_PE

PART
I

Teaching Primary School Gymnastics

Part I of this book discusses the importance of physical activity and how fundamental movement patterns in skill acquisition are categorised throughout this resource and the scheme of work featured on the bound-in DVD. Chapter 2 guides you through long-term, medium-term and short-term targets and all further aspects of planning and preparation to ensure that your gymnastics programme is efficient and complements the foundation stage early learning goals and the key stage 1 and key stage 2 primary National Curriculum guidelines. Chapter 3 promotes the use of hand apparatus and large apparatus in a gymnastics environment and outlines where the apparatus is used in the units of work. The chapter also offers guidelines on health and safety regarding the transport and use of the large apparatus and the importance of involving hand apparatus in a primary school gymnastics lesson. Chapter 4 discusses attainment and assessment.

CHAPTER

1

Developing Fundamental Movement Skills Through Gymnastics

This chapter explains the concept of fundamental movement skills and how they are used as actions in the gymnastics formula that is the basis of gymnastics skill acquisition in this teaching resource. Each fundamental movement skill that is used in the gymnastics formula throughout the book and DVD is explained in detail here. This chapter also describes how patterns of physical development and growth can influence the learning of gymnastics skills.

What Are Fundamental Movement Skills?

Fundamental movement skills are movement patterns that involve various body parts and provide the basis of physical literacy. Fundamental movement skills are the foundational movements, or precursor patterns, to the more specialised and complex skills used in play, games and specific sports. Physical literacy describes the ability of a person to instruct the body to perform an action accurately and with confidence and to recognize the physical, social, cognitive and emotional attributes required to do so effectively. Gymnastics-like activities promote the development of all movement patterns.

Fundamental movement skills feature predominantly through the units of work on the DVD and are referred to as action in the following gymnastics formula:

shape + action = gymnastics skill

Fundamental movement skills can be categorised into three groups: body management skills, locomotor skills and object control skills.

Body Management Skills

Body management skills involve balancing the body in stillness and in motion. Examples are static and dynamic balancing, rolling, landing, bending and stretching, twisting and turning, swinging, and climbing. The scheme of work on the DVD contains units of work that introduce, initiate and develop body management skills. Specific skills in the units include balancing (on large and small body parts, with a partner and in groups), rolling techniques, inversions, safe landings, and climbing. Body management skills can be developed using both the large apparatus and hand apparatus. Without competence in body management, the safe implementation and development of the other fundamental movement skills becomes difficult.

 Body management skills are featured throughout the units of work on the DVD in the Scheme of Work folder.

Locomotor Skills

Locomotor skills involve transporting the body in any direction from one point to another. Examples are crawling, walking, running, hopping, leaping, jumping, galloping, skipping and swimming. Several units of work on the DVD feature travelling skills and jumping and landing techniques. The themed games in chapter 11 of this book encourage exploring various ways to travel, and the Travel Techniques card in the Pictorial Resources folder on the DVD offers many ideas for varying modes of travelling. The Creature Movements resources complement most locomotor skills in fun and easy-to-instruct ways and are explained in chapter 11, Themed Games, and in the Themed Games folder within the Pictorial Resources folder on the DVD.

 Locomotor skills are featured throughout the units of work on the DVD in the Scheme of Work folder.

On the DVD, go to the Pictorial Resources folder. Refer to the Travel Techniques resource card

3

within the Flight and Travel subfolder. Also refer to the Creature Movements resource cards within the Themed Games folder.

Object Control Skills

Object control skills require controlling implements and objects such as balls, hoops, bats and ribbons by hand, by foot or with any other part of the body. Examples are throwing, catching, kicking, striking, bouncing and dribbling. The use of hand apparatus to promote object control skills and extend gymnastics activities is a theme present in all the units of work, which makes it unique in its approach to inclusive gymnastics. The activities offer a creative alternative to the direct learning of gymnastics-specific skills and provide an avenue through which to develop object control skills in a gymnastics environment.

 Object control skills are featured throughout the units of work on the DVD in the Scheme of Work folder.

Physical Development Patterns in Children

A child's physical appearance is very different to that of an adult, and there are many factors to be taken into consideration when instructing primary-aged children in gymnastics. Note the difference between an adult's physical appearance and a child's physical appearance (see figure 1.1).

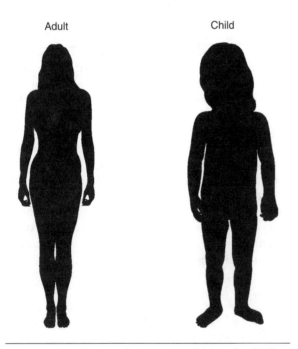

Adult   Child

Figure 1.1 Differences between an adult's and a child's physical appearance.

The proportions of the body change dramatically with age and growth; thus a child's entire skeletal structure is proportionally different to that of an adult. For example, a baby has a larger head and smaller limbs in comparison to the body of an adult. As a child grows and takes on the adult figure, the parts of the body do not grow at the same rate.

Note that body structure will determine behaviour patterns during a gymnastics lesson. Children with strong body frames will generally appear more confident and more likely to take risks when given large apparatus to climb on. Small children may encounter difficulties mounting and dismounting apparatus. On the other hand, large children may encounter difficulties when attempting to go under, over or around obstacles. Children with large heads and short arms will have difficulties in activities that require them to extend the arms above the head, such as the stretch roll. Children with short arms may also struggle to control hand apparatus because of the object's proximity to the torso.

From early infancy, movement acquisition follows a sequence of development based on the principles of cephalocaudal development; proximodistal development; and uni-, bi- and cross-lateral development. The progressive growth rate, cephalocaudal development (which means moving from head to foot), determines that control of the head develops first, then control of the torso and finally control of the lower limbs.

If we consider the implications of the cephalocaudal stages of development, it is reasonable to suggest that young children are more competent with rolling movement patterns and movement patterns close to the floor using multiple limbs than movement patterns that involve balancing or standing on one leg. A young child also might not be able to control basic motor skills in the legs, ankles and feet or have sufficient strength, coordination and balance to jump, land and dismount from large apparatus safely.

 See unit 3 (Encouraging Safe Dismounts), unit 7 (Jump, Land and Travel) and unit 11 (Flighted Foot Patterns) in the Scheme of Work folder on the DVD to encourage the development of lower-limb strength and maturity.

However, not only does the body grow in length; it also grows and develops in a central-to-peripheral direction. This is termed proximodistal development. A child gains control of body limbs in an inner-to-outer direction, that is, from the center of the body to its extremities. For example, the sequence of development for the arm goes from the shoulder to the arm to the wrist and then to the fingers. Finger dexterity (control) is the last to develop.

If you consider the implications of proximodistal development, you will observe that children initially learn to catch a ball by receiving it and hugging it to the body. That is, they gain control of the ball close to the midline of the body (the imaginary line that runs from the nose to the navel). It is a while before a child can reach out a hand and catch a ball at arm's length to the right or left of the midline. Young children characteristically demonstrate a lack of awareness or control when limbs are moved away from the midline of the body. This fact can be observed when young children are asked to carry out the activity of balancing beanbags on different parts of the body. Young children will characteristically demonstrate more control of the beanbag when it is placed on the shoulder rather than on the hand, which is extended away from the body.

Children will gain control of the body in a uni-, bi- and cross-lateral order. This means that they learn and take control of the limbs on the dominant side of the body first (uni-), then use the limbs on the less dominant side (bi-) and finally perform skills across the body (cross-lateral). An example is the backhand stroke in racquet sports. This development pattern is evident when observing young children controlling hand apparatus. They will use the dominant side to control the object, only rarely crossing the object across the body to the less dominant side.

Most gymnastics-like activities will aid the development of gross motor skills, which involve large movements and activity in the large muscle groups, such as rolling, jumping and travelling. Fine motor skills, which involve small, refined movements and require control using small muscle groups, include activities such as holding a pencil or wiggling the toes. It is also important to remember that no two children develop at exactly the same rate and development norms are only examples of average development rates.

Body Management Skills

Body management skills refer to the skills required for controlling and managing body movement patterns. In this teaching resource, the focus is on skills from the categories of balancing, climbing, inverting and rolling, from which you will learn gymnastics-specific skills explained in later chapters. The landing skill is considered a body management skill, but because I refer to landing as a consequence of jumping in all progressions in the scheme of work, an explanation of this skill is included in the locomotor skills section.

Balancing

Balance is a key development and is essentially the first of the fundamental movement skills to be established before successful progression to other key acquisitions of coordination and agility can occur. Without developing competence in balance, a child will struggle with learning to become coordinated in movement. The acquisition of balance focuses on learning to do a static balance and to understand what it is to be still. The body management and control required for a young child to maintain a static balance are immense and therefore will not be easy, but it will establish the foundations of learning to control the body and emphasize the importance of self-discipline.

To aid teachers in instructing early static balancing techniques, an understanding of the basic biomechanics of stability and balance would be beneficial. In simple terms, stability and balance are easier to achieve when the supporting base covers a large area. The larger, wider bases provide greater stability and are easier to balance on than smaller, narrower bases. Many bases (hands and feet) provide greater stability and allow for easier balance than fewer bases. Examples of the supporting base covering a large area include balancing on a large body part (see figure 1.2*a* on page 6) or balancing on multiple small body parts covering a large area. Examples of the supporting base covering a small area include balancing on one foot (see figure 1.2*b* on page 6).

The centre of mass is located in the middle of the body and responds to the pull of gravity (see figure 1.3 on page 6). The closer the centre of mass is to the floor, the easier it is to achieve stability and remain in balance. An example of a balance where the centre of mass is close to the base of support is a stretch shape on back. An example of a balance where the centre of mass is far away from the base of support is a stretch shape on feet.

Figure 1.4 on page 6 shows how the centre of mass stays in the middle of the body even though the body shape has altered. Notice in figure 1.5 on page 6 that the centre of mass, indicated by the dot on the photo, can even fall outside the body! If the centre of mass remains over the base area, it is easier to achieve stability and remain in balance than when the centre of mass falls outside the base area. Finally, attempting to achieve balance in an upright position is easier than attempting to achieve balance in an inverted (upside-down) position, as in figure 1.4.

 In the Pictorial Resources folder, refer to the *Where's My Centre of Mass?* file in the Basic Biomechanics folder.

Figure 1.2 *(a)* Supporting base covering a large area; *(b)* supporting base covering a small area.

Figure 1.3 The centre of mass is in the centre of the body.

Figure 1.4 The centre of mass is in the middle of the body even though the body shape has been altered.

Figure 1.5 The centre of mass has shifted outside the body in this position, but it remains central over the base area.

To help a child's understanding and attainment of balance, give the following teaching points. Repeat and rehearse them at all opportunities during the early learning of static balance skills. You can refer to these three key words as the balance formula:

- Control: Approach the balance in a slow and controlled manner.
- Focus: Look at something that is not moving.
- Tight: Think about making the muscles of the body tight and strong.

Specific balance skills and activities are featured in the following units of work:

- Unit 2: Basic Shapes and Balances
- Unit 5: Balances on Large and Small Body Parts Alongside Skipping
- Unit 8: Mix 'n' Mingle Balances
- Unit 9: Symmetry and Group Balances

- Unit 10: Partner Up and Roll
- Unit 12: Building Boxes and Bridges
- Unit 14: Push, Pull and Skip
- Unit 15: All Change

To challenge pupils' understanding when teaching principles of balancing, you can vary the task by using different body parts. By asking pupils to balance on various parts of the body, you reinforce their spatial awareness and body awareness and management skills.

Large body parts that can be used for balancing are the back, buttocks, shoulders, side, and belly (see figure 1.6, a-e). Small body parts that

Figure 1.6 Balances on large body parts: (a) back; (b) front (belly); (c) side; (d) buttocks; (e) shoulders.

can be used for balancing are the feet, hands, elbows, and knees. Balances that use a combination of small body parts are usually referred to as taking place on one, two, three or four points (see figure 1.7, *a-d*).

 In the Pictorial Resources folder, refer to the files titled Balances on Large Body Parts and Balances on Small Body Parts in the Balance Combinations folder. Also share figures 1.6 and 1.7 with your pupils.

Early attempts at the static balance often result in the following:

- The body wobbling around
- The body lacking stability
- The limbs waving about in an attempt to regain stability
- The eyes not focused on a still or permanent object

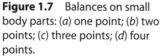

Figure 1.7 Balances on small body parts: (*a*) one point; (*b*) two points; (*c*) three points; (*d*) four points.

Climbing

Climbing is categorised as a body management skill, but the action of climbing builds on the early movement pattern of crawling in that both are locomotor activities in which the arms work in opposition with the legs. That is, the arms and legs proceed alternately in an asymmetrical pattern. Children who did not crawl as infants ("bottom shufflers") might find the coordination of climbing difficult. Climbing essentially involves ascent and descent and therefore offers the opportunity to use large apparatus such as the wall bars. A certain amount of strength in the hands, arms and upper body is required in order for a child to perform the climbing task.

Climbing is a skill that requires confidence. If the opportunity to develop climbing skills is not offered in the early years, it becomes a very difficult skill to acquire in later childhood, when sensitivity to heights and a lack of upper-body strength in relation to bodily growth present a far more challenging task. Climbing is also categorised in gymnastics as travelling.

 Opportunities to experience climbing activities are featured throughout the scheme of work on the DVD.

The wall bars are used in the following units of work:

- Unit 3: Encouraging Safe Dismounts
- Unit 4: Early Rolling Techniques and Climbing
- Unit 6: Basic Shapes, Additional Rolling Techniques and Climbing
- Unit 9: Symmetry and Group Balances
- Unit 11: Flighted Foot Patterns
- Unit 12: Building Boxes and Bridges
- Unit 14: Push, Pull and Skip
- Unit 16: Rock, Roll and Invert

A young child's first experience of climbing is often up and down the stairs at home. Most children usually attempt this by holding on with both hands, placing the leading foot on the step up and then pulling the trailing foot up to join the first foot. The hands then move onwards to the next step, and the process is repeated. This is known as the homologous stage. The next stage of climbing, the homolateral stage, occurs when the hand and foot on the same side of the body move together before the hand and foot on the other side of the body move. This type of movement pattern is typical of unilateral development, where the use of one side of the body is more dominant than the use of the other side.

The final stage of development in climbing is the cross-lateral stage, where the right hand and the left foot (left or right choice of limb is dependent on dominant side) precede the left hand and the right foot when ascending or descending. This demonstrates bilateral development, the equal use of both sides of the body.

Early movement patterns in the three stages of climbing may use any of the following progressions:

- From the body leaning towards the climbing frame to the body more balanced and controlled, parallel to the climbing frame
- From the climbing motion lacking rhythm (first arm and second arm, then first leg and second leg) to the climbing motion having more rhythm (first leg and same-side hand moves before second leg and same-side hand joins the first) to the climbing motion being rhythmic (left arm, right leg, then right arm, left leg)
- From hands gripping each rung tightly to the hands neatly holding and releasing each rung more confidently
- From both hands on the same level and using the arms to pull the body upwards, demonstrating a dominance of upper-body function in relation to lower-limb use as described in the cephalocaudal pattern of physical development to using the lower limbs more progressively by extending the knees to push the body upwards and finally to where the hands reach for the next rung and knees extend fully to push the body upwards
- From the body being flexed at the hips to the body being fully extended at the hips
- From the foot feeling for placement to more accurate foot placements that signify a smooth, continuous stepping action
- From the eyes focusing to where hands are gripping to the eyes focusing forwards and upwards away from hands

Inversion

An inversion skill occurs when the hips are raised above the level of the head. In gymnastics, the opportunity to invert the body occurs regularly, and these skills can be transferred from floor to large apparatus. When planning lessons, take into consideration that some children are genuinely scared to go upside down and some find it disorientating, causing them to lose stability and ultimately lose confidence. Some children also might not be physically strong enough to support their body weight either partially or wholly on their hands and arms in order to raise the hips overhead. In younger children, the arms might still be small in relation to the size of the head and torso, making it almost physically impossible for them to invert the body. Children can also achieve inversion by hanging upside down on the wall bars. Some children naturally go upside down on the wall bars, and it is usually those with more confidence and experience in inverting who do so.

Gymnastics-specific inversion techniques are discussed in chapter 9, Inversions. Specific inversion skills are featured in the following units of work:

- Unit 12: Building Boxes and Bridges
- Unit 16: Rock, Roll and Invert

You might see these early movement patterns in pupils:

- A reluctance to place the head lower than the hips
- A loss of balance and stability
- An unawareness of what other parts of the body are doing, resulting in untidy limbs

 In the Pictorial Resources folder, refer to the Bridge file, the Handstand Progressions file, and the Cartwheel Progressions file in the Inversions folder.

In the Dartfish Mediabooks folder, refer to the handstand progressions and the cartwheel progressions clips in the Inversions mediabook.

Rolling

Considering the cephalocaudal stages of development, it is reasonable to suggest that young children will be moderately successful with rolling movement patterns. Children love to roll, and it is one of the very first movement patterns they perform as infants. They learn to roll over, first from back to front (supine to prone) and then from front to back (prone to supine). Both types of rolls precede kneeling on hands and knees, crawling and sitting. Rolling techniques encourage use and understanding of personal space and

general space while developing a body awareness and spatial awareness within the safe confines of a singular activity. In terms of categories of gymnastics movement, rolling is both a travelling activity and an activity of rotation. Gymnastics-specific rolling techniques are discussed in chapter 8, Rolling Techniques.

Before you instruct early rolling techniques, an understanding of the basic biomechanics of rotation is beneficial. In simple terms, rotation occurs when the centre of mass moves outside the base area, which is evident in the initiation of all rolls. This is also the very reason some children are genuinely frightened to attempt the forward roll because they have to move out of balance, thus becoming unstable. In figure 1.8, the centre of mass moves out of the base area to initiate rotation. Figure 1.9 demonstrates how this movement can create rotation when learning the forward roll.

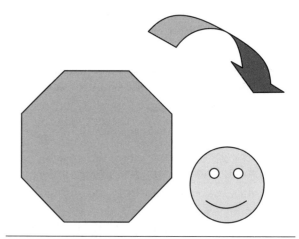

Figure 1.8 The centre of mass moves outside the base area. The smiling face depicts the centre of mass, and the hexagon depicts the base area.

Figure 1.9 The start of rotation in a forward roll, where the centre of mass has moved outside the base area of hands and feet, causing rotation to occur.

In the Pictorial Resources folder, refer to the Rotation file in the Basic Biomechanics folder.

Rolling techniques are featured in the following units of work:

- Unit 4: Early Rolling Techniques and Climbing
- Unit 6: Basic Shapes, Additional Rolling Techniques and Climbing
- Unit 10: Partner Up and Roll
- Unit 16: Rock, Roll and Invert

You will likely see these early movement patterns in rolling skills:

- Untidy or even lost shape of roll during movement pattern
- Untidy limbs resulting in bent legs, slack feet and bent arms
- Lumpy and irregular roll, not smooth and uniformed
- Roll performed in a crooked line (exception is the straddle roll)
- Lack of clear start and finish positions

 • In the Pictorial Resources folder, refer to the files in the Rolling Techniques folder.
- In the Dartfish Mediabooks folder, refer to the rolling techniques clips in the Rolling Techniques mediabook.

Locomotor Skills

Locomotor skills can be defined as any movement pattern that transports the body from one place to another place. Jumping and landing skills are reinforced early in the scheme of work as a safety aspect for dismounting apparatus, such as benches, and advance to run–jump–land progressions and onto basic vaulting techniques featured in unit 11, Flighted Foot Patterns. Locomotor skills can be varied, and many modes of travelling are included throughout the scheme of work, such as travelling in shapes, introduced in units 1, 3 and 7.

 In the scheme of work on the DVD, locomotor skills are explored through the themed game Creature Movements, which are featured in the following units of work:

- Unit 7: Jump, Land and Travel
- Unit 11: Flighted Foot Patterns

- Unit 15: All Change

Creature Movements resources are in the Themed Games folder in the Pictorial Resources folder.

Jumping and Landing

In young children, the joints and muscles of the lower extremities of the body (legs, feet and ankles) develop relatively late in comparison to the rest of the body. Pupils may need extra practice in activities such as jumping and landing on the floor before they can transfer those skills to the large apparatus.

Performing a jump requires maturity in leg strength to elevate the body off the ground against the force of gravity and coordination to synchronise the swinging of the arms upwards with the extension of the legs, resulting in an elevation from two feet to a landing on two feet. Dynamic balance is required for maintaining stability whilst the body is in motion and totally airborne.

Early movement patterns in jumping may include the following:

- Feet not parallel at start
- Attempting to elevate the body by leaning forward and bending at the hips but not bending the legs
- Poor and ineffective use of the arms
- One foot taking off the floor before the other when attempting to elevate the body
- The body moving forwards instead of vertically upwards in the flight phase
- A poor body shape during the flight phase
- Poor elevation during the jump
- One foot landing before the other after the flight phase
- Twisting in the body (asymmetry)
- Child looking at the floor for security
- Unstable landing

If a child has difficulty in jumping, it is possible to aid and support the child. Stand in front of the child and support him under the elbows; his arms should rest on your arms, and his hands should grip you at the elbow. Progress to holding at the child's wrists in the same way and then move to holding hands for support and confidence. Remember the child's arms and hands should always be on top of your arms and hands.

In addition to the physical support, verbally instruct, "Bend, jump, land," every time the child jumps, and demonstrate the bending of your legs as you aid the child to visually reinforce bending the legs to jump and land safely. It might be necessary to start learning to jump by jumping off a small elevation so that the force of gravity works with and not against the action of the jump.

The landing is the most important element of the jumping skill. You should initially teach it as a separate skill, enabling repetition and reinforcement. The majority of children's injuries occur during uncontrolled landings. Learning to land safely with competence will reduce the risk of injury to children and increase their confidence when learning new skills or when dismounting from the apparatus. Following are the key steps to the landing:

1. Prepare to land from a flighted action such as a jump by extending the body with arms raised above the head to reduce any rotation.

2. As the feet make contact with the landing surface, the impact is absorbed by the controlled flexion of the knees, ankles and hips while the arms move forwards to the horizontal position to adopt the landing position.

3. When the body is static, the legs should straighten, the hip angle should open and the body should return to an extended upright position (see figure 1.10a).

 In the Pictorial Resources folder, refer to the Spot Landing file in the Flight and Travel folder.

Early movement patterns in landing include the following:

- Body is not extended in flight before contact with the floor.
- Ankles, knees and hips do not flex at all on impact (child appears stiff-legged).
- Ankles, knees and hips flex too much so that assistance is needed from the hands and arms or the child finishes on buttocks.
- Poor body shape is caused by child focusing on the floor.
- Landing is unstable.

 Jumping and landing as a skill is featured in the following units of work on the DVD in the Scheme of Work folder:

- Unit 1: Space, Listening Pose, Movement Patterns and Basic Shapes
- Unit 3: Encouraging Safe Dismounts
- Unit 7: Jump, Land and Travel
- Unit 11: Flighted Foot Patterns

Running

Running, or a flighted elevation from one foot to the other, forms the basis of all flighted locomotor skills such as skips, chassés and leaps. As stated earlier, in young children, the joints and muscles of the lower extremities of the body (legs, feet and ankles) develop relatively late in comparison to

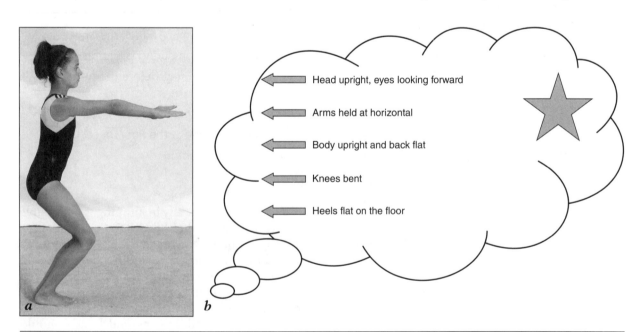

Figure 1.10 (a) The spot landing; (b) technical advice for the spot landing.

the rest of the body. Practice in toddling and walking gradually builds the asymmetrical movement skill and helps children develop awareness and the coordination pattern of gently swinging the arms to move in opposition to the legs. Children need to mature and develop sufficient strength in the large muscle groups around the hips and knees to be able to project the body from the ground, as in the action of running. The whole combination of actions need to be coordinated to ensure an efficient, fluent running motion. Running is the precursor to attempting more complex locomotor skills (such as skipping, side stepping, leaping), which could be included as pulse raisers (refer to chapter 5, Preparing For and Recovery From Physical Activity) in the warm-up at the beginning of lessons.

 Running as a skill is featured in the following units of work on the DVD in the Scheme of Work folder:

- Unit 3: Encouraging Safe Dismounts
- Unit 7: Jump, Land and Travel
- Unit 11: Flighted Foot Patterns

Following are some early motor patterns in the action of running:

- Upright body position
- Shoulders rotating from side to side during motion
- Head turning from side to side during motion
- Eyes not focused in direction of motion
- Slight or nonexistent flight phase
- Straight-legged gait, short leg swing or uneven stride
- Flat-footed action with flexed ankles
- Uncontrolled arm swinging, often swinging outwards horizontally
- Arms straight
- Arms and legs not always working in opposition
- Uneven rhythm

Once the basic locomotor skills of running and jumping have been mastered, more complex skills can be developed. Jumping skills develop into jumping patterns, such as jumping the feet out and in and hopscotch, or hopping and skipping. Running skills develop into side steps and chassé patterns or leaping and hurdling.

 Complex locomotor skills feature in unit 11: Flighted Foot Patterns on the DVD in the Scheme of Work folder.

Object Control Skills

Hand apparatus are included in most of the units of work on the DVD to allow children the opportunity to explore controlling and handling objects such as balls, beanbags, hoops, ribbons and skipping ropes.

Hand apparatus in a gymnastics lesson are vital components that promote the development of the object control skills whilst adding variety and encouraging creativity. The use of apparatus is attainable to most children and promotes self-confidence and self-esteem. Hand apparatus also promotes problem solving and creative thinking. For safety reasons, note that hand apparatus should be used only in floor-based activities and not taken onto the large apparatus. The individual pieces used in this teaching resource are available in most primary schools, and proper use of the hand apparatus is explained in more detail in chapter 3.

 Balls, beanbags, hoops, ribbons and ropes are featured in the following units of work on the DVD in the Scheme of Work folder:

- Balls feature in the following units of work:
  - Unit 4: Early Rolling Techniques and Climbing
  - Unit 8: Mix 'n' Mingle Balances
  - Unit 11: Flighted Foot Patterns
  - Unit 12: Building Boxes and Bridges
  - Unit 13: Mirror, Match and Canon
  - Unit 16: Rock, Roll and Invert
- Beanbags are featured in the following units of work and are used to reinforce the skill of balancing:
  - Unit 2: Basic Shapes and Balances
  - Unit 5: Balances on Large and Small Body Parts Alongside Skipping
  - Unit 8: Mix 'n' Mingle Balances
  - Unit 11: Flighted Foot Patterns
  - Unit 13: Mirror, Match and Canon
- Hoops are my favourite piece of hand apparatus, and I often include them in many floor-based activities. Hoops are featured in the following units of work:
  - Unit 3: Encouraging Safe Dismounts
  - Unit 6: Basic Shapes, Additional Rolling Techniques and Climbing

- Unit 8: Mix 'n' Mingle Balances
- Unit 11: Flighted Foot Patterns
- Unit 16 Rock, Roll and Invert
- Ribbons are the pupils' favourite because of the bright colours and fluid movement patterns. Ribbons are featured in the following units of work:
  - Unit 1: Space, Listening Pose, Movement Patterns and Basic Shapes
  - Unit 7: Jump, Land and Travel
  - Unit 8: Mix 'n' Mingle Balances
  - Unit 9: Symmetry and Group Balances
  - Unit 13: Mirror, Match and Canon
  - Unit 16: Rock, Roll and Invert
- Ropes are great to use as a means of increasing coordination and fitness in skipping activities. Skipping is featured in the following units of work:
  - Unit 3: Encouraging Safe Dismounts
  - Unit 5: Balances on Large and Small Body Parts Alongside Skipping
  - Unit 10: Partner Up and Roll
  - Unit 11: Flighted Foot Patterns
  - Unit 14: Push, Pull and Skip
  - Unit 15: All Change

Physical Literacy Skills

Physical literacy, which was introduced in the preface, is the ability to give the body an instruction and for the body then to perform the motion exactly as instructed.

 Unit 8, Mix 'n' Mingle Balances, demonstrates and promotes the importance of physical literacy, and it allows pupils to demonstrate their competence in the fundamental skill categories of body management skills, locomotor skills and object control skills.

The concept of physical literacy encourages pupils to solve problems by translating verbal or visual instructions into physical actions that challenge both balance and coordination skills. The activity tasks are carried out with a partner, which encourage cooperative communication skills and promote teamwork. Unit 8, Mix 'n' Mingle Balances, can be both challenging and attainable and, above all, great fun.

The tasks are listed according to named body parts, and subsequent partner tasks fall into three categories:

1. Small body parts (such as a balance on two knees, one hand, one foot; see figure 1.11a)
2. Large body parts (such as a balance on both pupils' buttocks; see figure 1.11b)
3. A mix of small and large body parts (such as a balance on the entire back and two feet; see figure 1.11c)

 In the Pictorial Resources folder, refer to the Mix 'n' Mingle Balances file in the Balance Combinations folder.

You can progressively extend Mix 'n' Mingle by adding one or two pieces of hand apparatus to develop object control skills. Locomotor skill development is encouraged when the task involves composing short sequences.

Physical literacy ideas can also be used as pulse raisers in key stage 2 warm-up activities; refer to chapter 11 for those ideas.

Figure 1.11 Mix 'n' Mingle balances: (*a*) small body parts; (*b*) large body parts; (*c*) small and large body parts.

Ensuring Effective Delivery of Gymnastics in Primary Education

As with all lessons in the key areas of learning within the primary curriculum, you will benefit greatly if you are well prepared. Gymnastics is no exception. This chapter details how this teaching resource is planned to provide you with an efficient progressive gymnastics programme to deliver to your pupils during their time in primary education.

Complete Guide to Primary Gymnastics fulfils the purpose and aims of the early learning goals in the foundation stage and the primary National Curriculum for physical education. This chapter maps the links between the skills and activities suggested in the units on the DVD and the key aspects of learning from the early learning goals and National Curriculum guidelines. Each unit also provides cross-curricular suggestions and information, communication and technology tasks to ensure that learning through gymnastics encompasses all areas of the National Curriculum and is relevant to daily activities.

Planning for Gymnastics in Primary Education

When planning your gymnastics programme you should address three questions:

1. What are you trying to achieve?
2. How will you organise learning?
3. How will you know when you are achieving your aims?

In this teaching resource, planning takes the form of meeting targets through long-term, medium-term and short-term planning.

Long-Term Planning

The scheme of work on the DVD contains a curriculum in the key activity area of gymnastics in physical education for primary school pupils (reception through year 6). The long-term plan meets the guidelines of the early learning goals and primary National Curriculum.

A long-term plan focuses on the targets you would like your pupils to achieve by the end of the programme. The long-term plan therefore ensures that pupils have acquired the physical attributes to achieve a reasonable level of skill in gymnastics and the knowledge to extend gymnastics tasks in a meaningful way with a view towards evaluating and improving performances, thus preparing them for participation in gymnastics in year 7 at secondary school. The scheme of work on the DVD details many procedures, such as building on basics, the introduction of partner work, and tasks based on themed ideas to ensure the continued acquisition of knowledge and skill.

The long-term plan demonstrates how the units of work on the DVD are distributed across the foundation stage and key stage 1 and key stage 2 periods in a sequence that promotes curriculum continuity and progress in pupils' learning. Supporting the principle that gymnastics activities have wide-reaching benefits, different aspects of the units of work are cross-curricular, linking with other key areas of learning in the national curriculum. Your long-term plan should answer this question: What are you trying to achieve?

Medium-Term Planning

Medium-term planning takes into account the methods you can employ to reach your long-term targets. Think of the medium-term plans as the stepping stones to achieving your long-term targets. In this scheme of work, the medium-term plans can be identified as the targets you would like your pupils to achieve by the end of the foundation stage, key stage 1 and key stage 2.

By the end of the foundation stage, pupils will have acquired a repertoire of elementary movement skills through simple physical coordination activities involving body management tasks, locomotor skills and object control skills centred on basic gymnastics activities that enable them to become competent movers with an understanding of simple rules that ensure that they are responsible for their actions. Attainment of the skills and knowledge will enable pupils in key stage 1 to focus on further skill development introducing gymnastics-specific skills learnt through the gymnastics formula and through observation. They will learn to value the performances of others so that by the end of the key stage they understand how their bodies work and what skills and movement patterns they can achieve. In key stage 2 those previously learnt skills become channelled into themed units of work that challenge pupils to extend their learning through partner and group work and to use those skills in creative and meaningful ways, thus meeting the long-term targets.

The individual units of work build on pupils' experience and ability, enabling the use of progressive activities that meet the requirements of the National Curriculum and plan towards achieving the long-term target. Your medium-term plan through implementing the scheme of work in *Complete Guide to Primary Gymnastics* answers this question: How will you organise learning?

Short-Term Planning

The short-term plan involves the steps and procedures you will take to meet your medium-term and ultimately long-term plans and targets. Short-term planning in *Complete Guide to Primary Gymnastics* refers to the individual units of work featured on the DVD. Each unit of work contains instruction for the basic structure of the gymnastics lessons and details the learning intentions and learning outcomes explained in the overview at the beginning of each unit. A focus on learning through a progression of lessons will enable pupils to meet the short-term targets identified in the learning objectives. The learning objectives are varied, giving pupils many opportunities to demonstrate their understanding and achievements through avenues such as acquisition of gymnastics skills, creative movement patterns, open discussion, evaluating and improving techniques, question-and-answer tasks and problem-solving initiatives. Your short-term plan should answer this question: How will you know when you are achieving your aims?

If you wish to take gymnastics instruction further than the curriculum-based activities, *Complete Guide to Primary Gymnastics* and its scheme of work on the DVD provide an excellent foundation and insight into teaching gymnastics. It provides a clear understanding of the basics for teachers' continued professional develop-

ment (CPD). For further information regarding teaching courses and qualifications, contact your national governing body for gymnastics. (In the UK, awards for teachers are offered by the national governing body British Gymnastics [www.british-gymnastics.org] and UK Gymnastics [www.ukgymnastics.net]).

Learning In and Through Gymnastics

In most cases, pupils approach physical activity lessons willingly, displaying high levels of enthusiasm. After all, this is only an extension of play! The scheme of work on the DVD ensures that gymnastics is a fun, relevant and attainable form of structured play. The individual units of work are displayed in figure 2.1.

Implementing the Foundation Stage: Early Learning Goals for Physical Education

The following are early learning goals for physical development in the foundation stage (Statutory Framework for the Early Years Foundation Stage, Department for Education and Skills 2007):

- **Move with confidence and imagination and in safety.** The foundation stage units of work 1 to 4 provide the opportunity to learn the basic shapes used in gymnastics and to explore the actions that contribute to the gymnastics formula that is the basis for learning gymnastics skills. This knowledge will allow children to move with confidence and imagination and in safety.

- **Move with control and coordination.** Teaching pupils gymnastics-specific shapes and movement patterns provides flexible barriers for encouraging skills that demonstrate control and coordination throughout the units of work in the foundation stage.

- **Travel around, under, over and through balancing and climbing equipment.** The four units of work for the foundation stage include activities that involve using large apparatus such as platforms, benches and wall bars; these apparatus encourage the children to travel around, under, over and through balancing and climbing equipment.

- **Show awareness of space, of themselves and of others.** In this resource, the importance of children's showing an awareness

Learning In and Through Gymnastics

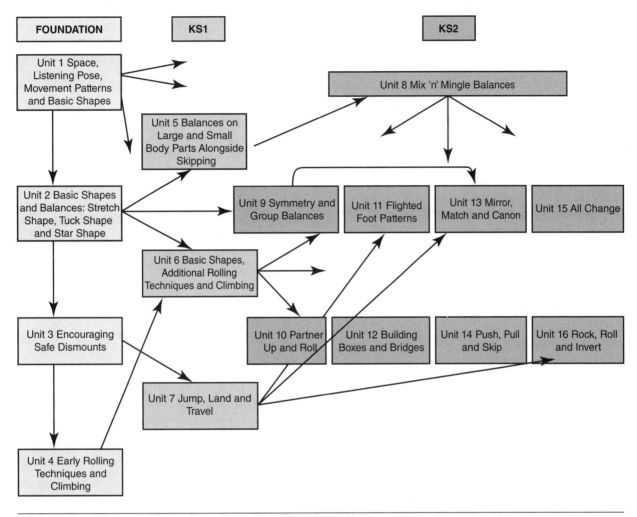

Figure 2.1 Progressions through the units of work in each stage of primary physical education.

of space, of themselves and of others is reinforced. Unit 1 in the scheme of work is all about the learning of this application.

- **Recognise the importance of keeping healthy and those things that contribute to this.** The foundation stage units of work encourage a discussion of recognising the importance of keeping healthy and suggests encouraging discussion before and after the lesson when either preparing the children for the activity or recapping events after the lesson.

- **Recognise the changes that happen to their bodies when they are active.** The teaching points in each unit of work for the foundation stage provide discussion and activities to help children recognise the changes that happen to their bodies when they are active.

- **Use a range of small and large equipment.** Every unit of work has activities that use hand apparatus and large apparatus,

fulfilling the requirement of this early learning goal.

- **Handle tools, objects, construction and malleable materials safely and with increasing control.** All the hand apparatus used in the foundation stage units of work meet the requirements of this early learning goal through the handling of tools and objects with increasing control that is required for fulfilling the task.

Implementing the National Curriculum: Four Key Aspects of Learning in Key Stage 1 and Key Stage 2

Notes taken from QCDA (2010).

The key area of learning for physical education in the National Curriculum is to acquire knowledge, skills and understanding in a physically active environment through four strands of learning. Acquiring and developing skills, selecting and applying skills, evaluating and improving skills and knowledge and understanding of fitness and health are implemented into the scheme of work on the DVD.

Acquiring and Developing Skills

Acquiring and developing skills involve learning basic skills and building up through progressions. Acquiring and developing skills, in a broad sense, are about pupils becoming aware of themselves and their bodies during patterns of movement. At the beginning of all units of work and individual lessons, there should be a focus on acquiring new skills and developing previously learnt skills to establish basic gymnastics skills that can be used as tools to facilitate the learning of more progressive gymnastics skills and complex sequences. It is very important that the fundamentals of gymnastics such as the basic gymnastics shapes and postural shapes be introduced in the foundation stage and key stage 1 (see figure 2.2), repeated and rehearsed initially so that they can then be applied to the actions of balancing (individually or in pairs), jumping and landing, rolling, inverting, climbing and travelling, as instructed in all the stages.

Teaching skill development across key stages can help pupils do the following:

- Explore, develop and establish basic movement patterns and actions.
- Develop coordination and control of their bodies, increasing their range of movement of gross and fine motor skills.
- Move spontaneously and improvise in a range of physical activities.

- Provide a pool of basic skills from which further development and progression in gymnastics can be built.

Selecting and Applying Skills, Tactics and Compositional Ideas

This key aspect involves selecting the learnt skills and applying them into compositional routines, focusing on entrances, exits and linking skills both as individuals and in groups (see figure 2.3). Selecting and applying skills require pupils to select the gymnastics skills that they have learnt and to apply them to a particular purpose using a variety of tactics and compositional ideas. In gymnastics instruction, you can achieve this by adopting the simple formula to build up gymnastics-specific skills:

shape + action = gymnastics skill

By adopting the same gymnastics formula of shape + action = gymnastics skill, you can transfer basic gymnastics shapes or learnt gymnastics skills onto the large apparatus.

Finally, learnt gymnastics skills can be selected and applied in composing simple and complex sequences. Teaching this aspect across key stages can help pupils to do the following:

- Make informed choices regarding gymnastics skills (what to do and how to do it).
- Perform and then combine and sequence actions.
- Apply, follow and understand rules that govern specific roles in gymnastics activities (such as symmetrical shapes and canoning).
- Use equipment safely for a specific purpose.

Figure 2.2 *(a)* Basic gymnastics shapes and *(b)* postural shapes form the first part of the gymnastics formula.

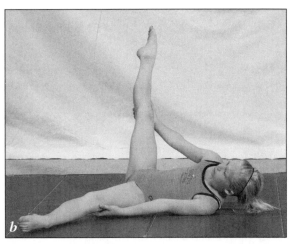
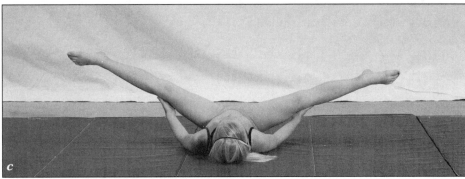

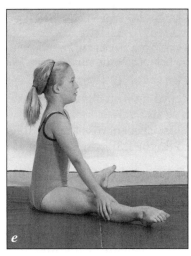

Figure 2.3   The principles of the gymnastics formula: *(a)* straddle shape + *(b-e)* rolling action = straddle roll.

Evaluating and Improving Performance

The key aspect of evaluating and improving considers technical points, presentation skills and inclusion with a view towards evaluating and improving one's own as well as others' performance. I think that this key learning aspect should read evaluate–improve–re-evaluate. To evaluate a gymnastics skill or gymnastics activity is essentially to judge the competence of the performance. To do that, you need an understanding of technical knowledge, which can be acquired through the resource cards located on the DVD where technical advice is given and the correct use of vocabulary and language is highlighted in the speech bubbles, promoting set criteria of evaluation points by which a performance can be judged (see figure 2.4). Correct vocabulary is essential, and gymnastics has a language of its own. Once a performance has been evaluated and improved according to set criteria, the performance should be re-visited in order to monitor and evaluate the attainment. Gymnastics activities can be evaluated and

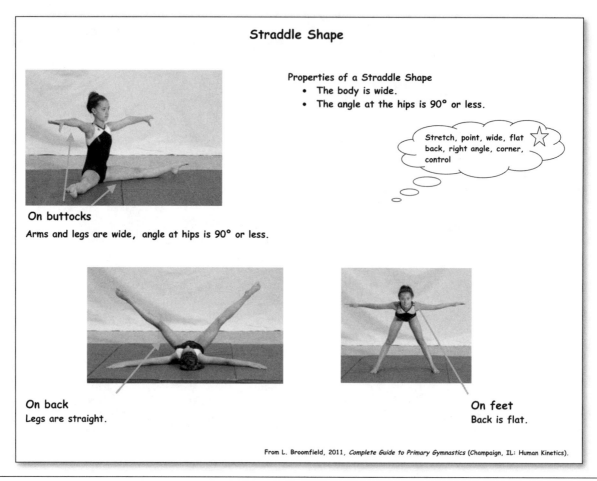

Figure 2.4 Gymnastics activities can be evaluated and improved according to technical accuracy and presentation skills, and this is an example of how the resource cards will appear on the bound-in DVD.

improved according to technical accuracy and presentation skills.

Teaching this aspect across the key stages can help pupils to do the following:

- Improve the quality of their performance and presentation.
- Develop their skills in communicating thoughts about a gymnastics activity.
- Develop their listening skills and the ability to collaborate with others.
- Enter a debate and understand the benefits incurred from the sharing of ideas when exploring various options.
- Become aware of the needs of others when observing and providing feedback.
- Appreciate and acknowledge others' good work in gymnastics performances.
- Recognise and cope with personal success and limitations in their ability to perform gymnastics skills.
- Use correct gymnastics-specific vocabulary.

In the units of work on the DVD, the stars and wishes system of evaluating and improving

a performance amongst peers offers a positive approach within set criteria. When pupils observe a performance, I ask them to share two star points they really enjoyed watching in the

Ideas to Help Implement Evaluating and Improving Performances

- Encourage and employ start and finish positions throughout.
- Explore the use of legs, arms and head in creative ways.
- Focus on and discuss the accuracy of technical points.
- Plan simple but effective links when sequencing.
- Concentrate on body management and control.
- Use planned and rehearsed movement patterns.

performance. They also must share one wish of what they would like to see done differently next time to improve that moment. These may be technical points, creative ideas or presentation skills.

Knowledge and Understanding of Fitness and Health

Knowledge and understanding of fitness and health involve understanding the environmental requirements, body preparation and benefits associated with undertaking the skills safely. Knowledge and understanding of fitness and health begin with a willingness and desire to be physically active and an inspired interest in learning how the body works and the ensuing benefits of leading an active and healthy lifestyle.

Teaching this aspect across key stages can help pupils to do the following:

- Become aware of the range of activities necessary for their own health and well-being, including eating habits, sleeping patterns, and hygiene.

- Establish and develop positive attitudes about exercise and regularly taking part in physical activity.

- Understand the importance of preparation for and recovery from exercise and activity, including the the purpose and importance of warming up and cooling down.

- Develop an educated awareness of the body's skeletal and muscular structures, including functions of the skeleton and names of bones, names of functions of muscles and the role of joints.

- Develop an awareness of the physiological changes that occur to the body during exercise and activity, including change in respiration, change in temperature, change in circulation and rate of heart beat and the impact that exercise has on muscle length (associations with flexibility exercises and strengthening activities).

- Understand the long-term benefits associated with exercise and activity (for example, physical activity strengthens bones and muscles and improves the range of motion in joints).

- Understand basic health and safety guidelines, including transportation, erection and dismantling of large apparatus and safe practice concerning suitable exercises.

- Develop an understanding of emotional responses, such as how exercise makes people feel and whether people's mood can affect the way they move.

- Develop an understanding of social cooperation and teamwork.

Linking Information and Communication Technology With Gymnastics

Information and communication technology (ICT) can help pupils learn and improve their experience in physical education. In gymnastics, pupils can improve efficiency and evaluate work by communicating with others through the presentation of information. Data from gymnastics activities can be collected, analysed and interpreted. Pupils can access information to enhance learning in and through physical education through such topics as anatomy, physiology, sport in society, health and well-being. ICT allows pupils, especially those who are unable to be physically active, to learn through roles other than that of the performer.

Information and communication technology in gymnastics offers pupils the opportunity to support their work by being taught to do the following tasks:

- Source information and use this knowledge to enhance their understanding of a task.

- Develop ICT skills to refine and enhance the accuracy of their work.

- Present and share information directly and through electronic media.

- Review, modify and evaluate their work, reflecting critically on its quality as it progresses.

ICT can be implemented in a gymnastics lesson in a variety of ways. The following hardware and software items can be used with a view towards planning, administration, teaching and reviewing:

- Pupils can access the Internet to gain information from a variety of sources around the world (restrictions need to be applied by schools to limit access only to known and reputable sites).

- Primary schools may have their own intranet where pupils can access information from within a school's own site, which is a safe way to allow pupils to search for information within boundaries set by each school.

- Much information, such as that included in this teaching resource, comes on a DVD that, when inserted into a computer, can be shared with others.
- Other software packages allow pupils to collect, collate, analyse and present information in the form of a text document, a graphics document, a picture document or a combination of these sources, such as a poster or a slide presentation.
- Equipment may involve digital cameras and videos, which record images that can be displayed directly via a computer and edited and stored for future reference.

Visual learning is a tool that enhances learning. This is evident in such a visual activity as gymnastics and one that is valued by me and used extensively throughout *Complete Guide to Primary Gymnastics*. Use of an interactive whiteboard is a tool that has the potential to improve teaching and learning through presentation, demonstration and modelling techniques that actively engage pupils. As with the use of all equipment, ensure that you discuss with all pupils the guidelines for usage and that they understand those guidelines. Regarding the use of cameras and videos, give careful consideration to all child protection issues and respect all personal requests from pupils and their families.

When implementing ICT tasks into a gymnastics lesson, remember that the lesson is primarily a physical education lesson and you and your pupils should not be over burdened with the ICT facts. Therefore the ICT tasks should assist, enhance and progress pupils' learning in gymnastics. Ensure that pupils can carry out each ICT task before involving gymnastics activities.

Inclusion and Differentiation Objectives

It is a statutory requirement to provide pupils with relevant and appropriately challenging work at each stage. The National Curriculum sets out three principles of developing a more inclusive curriculum (QCDA 2010):

- **Setting suitable learning challenges.** Learning challenges can be adapted to meet individual needs through differentiation, as explained in this section.
- **Responding to pupils' diverse learning needs.** Diverse learning needs may include race, gender or cultural factors.

- **Overcoming potential barriers to learning and assessment for individuals and groups of pupils.** Potential barriers may include special educational needs, physical disabilities or learning English as a second language.

To ensure a gymnastics lesson is inclusive, it will be necessary to adopt principles of differentiation. Differentiation is solely concerned with the properties of adaptation. Planning for differentiation should cover the following:

- Pupil groupings based on ability, activity and pupil requirements
- Resources (equipment, space, time)
- Pupil activity based on tasks, pupil roles and responsibility
- Other opportunities (such as extra-curricular activities, club links)

Differentiation can be done by task or by outcome. Differentiation by task is achieved when pupils who are pursuing the same learning objectives are given various but related tasks according to levels of ability and understanding. Following are some examples of differentiation by task on an individual basis: a large apparatus may be adapted by changing the height, distance or composition; a hand apparatus may be adapted by size, weight or sound; and skills can be broken down into components and progressive steps. Some examples of differentiation by task in a small-group situation may require pupils to take the responsibility of different roles, including observation, data collection, equipment monitoring or officiating or coaching.

Differentiation by outcome involves setting tasks that are suitable and appropriate for a pupil's starting level and allow progress to be made. For example, in gymnastics, basic gymnastics shapes are attainable to most children, but a more able child would be able to select a shape and use it in more challenging ways than a less able performer.

Class Management and Organisation

Before the commencement of any physical activity lesson, appropriate risk assessments should be carried out. Risk assessment involves managing the risk, or possibility of injury. In the context of physical activity, risk assessment involves providing a balance between appropriate challenge and an acceptable level of risk:

appropriate challenge = appropriate risk

Following are factors that affect the balance of this equation:

- **The people involved such as teaching staff, pupils, coaches and volunteers.** They should be qualified by being sufficiently skilled, competent and confident to carry out tasks involved. Adults should demonstrate and reinforce acceptable patterns of behaviour and discipline and demonstrate effective observation and communication techniques. They should be appropriately supervised for tasks involved (adequate adult-to-pupil ratio), and they must have knowledge of the curriculum. Adults should understand their obligations relating to duty of care.
- **The context, including facility and equipment.** Operating procedures are known and applied and all safety rules and regulations are understood by both pupils and staff. The area of use is appropriate: adequate space, light and heating; non-slip floor; no obstructions. The equipment is regularly and systematically maintained, is appropriate for class and used for appropriate activities.
- **The organisation and teaching style of the activity.** For example, group organisation and management procedures are in place, such as registers, and a comprehensive scheme of work offers differentiation to meet the needs of all pupils. Pupils are prepared and informed to carry out tasks which match their capability (preparation and progressions are understood and applied).

For detailed explanations on assessing risk, refer to the Association for Physical Education, *Safe Practice in Physical Education and School Sport* (2008), by Peter Whitlam and Glen Beaumont.

When planning a gymnastics lesson, you can break it down into three sections: pre-activity preparation, main activity instruction, and post-activity tasks.

Pre-Activity

Pre-activity preparation will primarily involve deciding which unit of work you are going to use for the next block of lessons. Having decided on a unit of work, take the time to plan the lesson and gather the necessary pictorial resources and video clips on the DVD that support your chosen unit of work. The chosen unit of work should be outlined to your pupils before the commencement of any physical activity (perhaps in the classroom using the pictorial resources and video clips). An adage relates to the way teachers ought to sequence their teaching: "Tell them what you are going to tell them . . . tell them . . . tell them what you told them!" In other words, inform pupils about what they are going to learn. Pupils should be reminded of expected codes of conduct and behaviour. Reinforce the safety and the correct transportation, erection, dismantling and storage of apparatus, and highlight the possible outcomes of incorrect management. Information regarding the use of apparatus is in chapter 3, Using Apparatus in Primary Gymnastics.

Both you and your pupils should wear appropriate clothing at all times. You should be suitably attired to be mobile without restriction. Pay careful attention to clothing and footwear. Pupils should be dressed according to school PE kit policy (normally shorts and T-shirts for indoor activities) with bare feet. Long hair should be tied away from the face to prevent any distraction or disturbance to vision. This is a very important issue, and in fact I have prevented pupils with unsecured hair access to the apparatus, stressing safety above fashion. Pupils should not wear jewellery, and neither should you.

Main Activity

The lesson progressions in each unit of work on the DVD will guide you during the activity. It is important to lead by example regarding expected standards of behaviour and discipline and to establish and maintain ground rules of behaviour early on. Be alert to potential problems within the group's characteristics and abilities in gymnastics skills, particularly when grouping.

Always be active and involved, and above all be enthusiastic. If you are a teacher who is not confident in instructing gymnastics, try to overcome that by focusing on positive body language activities. Body language is vital to the overall impression and enthusiasm for the lesson. Demonstrate the following behaviour patterns, because they are interpreted as being positive and caring. When imparting instructions or listening to an individual or small group, get down to the participants' level, showing interest and ensuring eye contact. Always be active and energetic and use verbal and visual aids to instruct the pupils. When offering instructions, avoid sitting down, folding your arms, yawning or standing with your hands on your hips because these behaviour patterns can be interpreted as negativity and disinterest.

You should also avoid inactivity and staying in the same place in the hall. Walk around! I do this all the time to ensure that that the pupils are fully engaged. Even though you might be constantly on the move, ensure that you can observe and be observable to the whole group and that all the group can clearly see and hear you at all times. (For example, be aware of the position of the sun in relation to your standing in the hall.) Never turn your back on the class.

Give instructions that are clear and precise. That is, use vocabulary suitable to your pupils' age and ensure that pupils understand what is being asked of them by asking them to repeat the instructions. Effective communication is vital to the safety, understanding and teaching and learning of gymnastics skills. Always make your feedback positive, focusing on skills that are technically good and creative whilst praising leadership and cooperative teamwork. Try to instruct pupils on what they should do and not what they shouldn't do. The "stars and wishes" system of evaluating and improving a performance amongst peers, described earlier in this chapter, offers a positive approach within set criteria. Goals help to focus their attention, so keep returning to the learning intentions at the beginning of each unit of work as you advance through the progressions.

Regarding physical demonstrations, gymnastics is a very physical activity. Actions speak louder than words, and if you would prefer not to or are unable to perform a physical demonstration, you might ask a pupil to demonstrate (one whom you know to be competent in the gymnastics skill and perhaps attends gymnastics classes outside of school). Remember, though, you will also have prepared from the DVD your visual pictorial resources and short video clips to ensure visual learning opportunities are available in most cases, so use them! Above all, remember that most pupils enjoy gymnastics!

The lesson should follow a structured outline (introduction, development, conclusion), such as the following example:

- Outline the objectives of the lesson.
- Conduct a warm-up.
- Transport and erect required apparatus.
- Session activities should meet either early learning goals or the four key aspects of learning in key stage 1 or key stage 2.
- Dismantle apparatus.
- Conduct a cool-down session. You can also conduct the cool-down session before dismantling the apparatus.
- Review, appraise and evaluate session.

Involving non-performers is very important. Occasionally you will have pupils who are unable to participate in the gymnastics lesson, perhaps because of illness or injury. Include those pupils in activities relating to the lesson, such as taking responsibility for the information and communi-

cation technology (ICT) task for that unit of work which will be of value and benefit to themselves and participants. Another way of incorporating non-performers is to involve them in the planning and evaluating activities of the lesson, ensuring that they engage with the intended learning objectives, albeit in a different way. Following are learning opportunities for non-performers:

- Helping a partner or small group to plan a short gymnastics sequence
- Helping devise tactics to solve problems
- Acting as a coach with a group, using teaching points that you provide
- Helping to plan apparatus layout for a future lesson
- Using gymnastics-specific vocabulary and appropriate language, describing an observed activity
- Providing feedback on observed performances
- Recording the performances with the use of photography or video

Post-Activity: Teacher's Evaluation of Lesson

You should regularly evaluate the lessons and your own performance to ensure that you are constantly delivering high-quality activities. Good evaluations should be focused, analytical and reasonable. You should record both successes and failures and be informative, which will influence future planning and teaching. The following is a checklist of questions that you can use as a self-evaluation regarding the three main areas of a gymnastics lesson (Based on Bailey, 2001).

Regarding the content of the lesson, here is the first point you should address: Was I prepared with the resources and subject knowledge to teach this lesson? If yes, then assess whether and how many of the pupils achieved the learning objectives outlined in your introduction to the lesson. If the answer to this is *only a few* or *none*, then you need to address further issues. For example, were the activities and tasks appropriate, and were the progressions suitable for pupils with varying abilities? Did they build progressions based on previous learning and experience, and was your feedback constructive and positive? Did you map the lesson accordingly with an introduction, a development and a conclusion stage?

Evaluating your organisation will take into account your pupils, space and time. Successful organisation of pupils can be paramount to effective learning and is a point that might need to be addressed throughout your lesson regarding discipline and behaviour, not just at the end during your evaluation. Did you include all non-performers (did you employ them with meaningful tasks that are appropriate for the learning objectives)? Consider your physical area: Was the required apparatus easily accessible? When it was erected, was there enough space for pupils to perform and move around the area safely? Were you always visible to the pupils? Did you allow enough practice time at each task for pupils to fully engage? If assistants were present, did you employ them in meaningful tasks?

Presentation is important because it sets the standards for learning. First, ask whether you and your pupils were dressed appropriately. Did you give instructions relevant to the age and ability of your pupils, and were resources available and appropriate? Did you present your instructions precisely in a clear voice and with positive body language? Finally, did you show enthusiasm?

For more information on assessment and achievement of your pupils, refer to chapter 4.

Hopefully you will feel confident to begin your gymnastics lessons with enthusiasm. Remember to plan your lessons, inform all pupils of the tasks ahead of time and reinforce expectations regarding behaviour and health and safety matters. By following the progressions in the unit of work that you have chosen, you will ensure that the lessons include an introduction, a development stage and a conclusion. Refer to chapter 5, Preparation For and Recovering From Physical Activity, for more information on the introduction and conclusion to gymnastics lessons. During the lesson, be active and adopt positive body language, demonstrating clear and precise communication skills. Remember to provide positive feedback and involve all non-performers. Afterwards, evaluate your lesson and reflect on areas to develop.

Using Apparatus in Primary Gymnastics

This chapter presents the use of apparatus in primary gymnastics. Throughout the resource, the apparatus used is referred to as either large apparatus or hand apparatus, and it is featured in all units of work for reception (year R) to year 6. The large apparatus identified throughout this resource is considered to be basic; therefore most of the named apparatus will be available to most primary schools. Hand apparatus is a vital component that adds variety to the lesson, requires little supervision, promotes the development of object control skills (fundamental movement skills), encourages creativity, and is attainable to most children, thereby promoting self-confidence and self-esteem.

Using Large Apparatus

The large apparatus used throughout the units of work on the DVD are mats, benches, platforms and wall bars. If access to the large apparatus is limited, modify the suggested activity stations shown in the apparatus outlays listed at the end of some units of work on the DVD. If your school has access to more large apparatus and space than are suggested in the planned apparatus outlays, you are encouraged to implement those pieces into the activity stations, thus providing more choice and enabling more activities.

You should follow the guidelines for safe practice and check with your own school policies and local authority before commencing a gymnastics lesson. You should also assess all lessons for risk before commencement. For detailed explanations on the use, transportation, erection and dismantling of large apparatus refer to the Association for Physical Education, *Safe Practice in Physical Education and School Sport* (2008), by Peter Whitlam and Glen Beaumont.

Mats

Mats are used throughout the scheme of work to provide a safe environment for performing gymnastics skills such as rolls, inversions, paired balances and jump and land activities. The use of mats is readily employed in most units of work. The following points should be used as a guideline with regards to the use of mats in a gymnastics environment.

Mats should be used only for gymnastics-specific skills such as rolls, inversions and paired balances. Also, when pupils execute jump dismounts, mats should also be used for absorbing the landings.

Here are a few facts to consider regarding the use of mats:

- Mats do not need to be used around or under large apparatus just in case a child might fall. Pupils should not be subjected to a false sense of security; that is, they should not think that mats offer them protection. If there is a concern with an apparatus setup or an activity that might result in a pupil falling, either the apparatus or the activity should be modified to reduce the risks and accurately reflect a pupil's capability.
- Mats will not prevent the breaking of a bone on an unexpected awkward landing. Mats are not a fail-safe protection system. Only the correct technical execution of a landing will prevent injury, and this should be emphasised to pupils regularly.
- The placing of mats in inappropriate places may encourage a pupil to take unnecessary risks such as jumping down from the wall bars instead of climbing down in a controlled manner.
- The excessive use of mats where it is not expected that pupils will need to cushion deliberate landings may serve as a real danger to young pupils; that is, extra mats can provide extra obstacles that pupils could trip over. Each mat should be placed for a specific purpose.

The following six steps encourage the safe transport of gymnastics mats:

1. Two pupils need to be positioned on each long side of the mat (see figure 3.1a).
2. When lifting up or placing down the mat, lifters should not bend the body at the hips

(see figure 3.1*b*). The body should remain upright and the knees should bend accordingly (see figure 3.1*c*).

3. Thumbs should be on the top of the mat when it is gripped (see figure 3.1*d*).

4. The mat should be transported at approximately waist height (see figure 3.1*e*).

5. Encourage all the pupils to face forward, looking and walking forward in the direction of travel (see figure 3.1*f*).

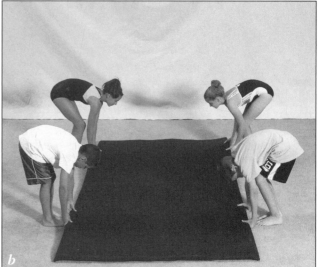

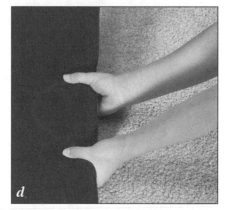

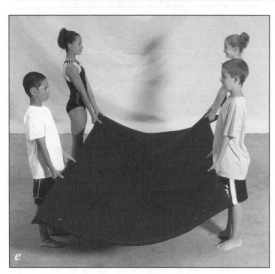

Figure 3.1 Proper carriage and transportation of mats: *(a)* positioning of pupils about to transport a gymnastics mat; *(b-c)* the incorrect and correct ways to position the body when attempting to lift up or place down a gymnastics mat; *(d)* placement of thumbs on top of a mat during transport; *(e)* height at which the gymnastics mat should be transported: below the waist; *(f)* direction that all lifters should face when transporting a gymnastics mat: forwards in the direction of travel.

6. Ensure a clear passage for the transport of the mats from the storage area to the activity station.

Benches

Benches are a versatile piece of large apparatus, which most schools have readily available for use. The units of work include the use of benches to develop skills in the categories of balance, inversion, travel, and jump and land. In the foundation stage and key stage 1, benches are used in specific units of work for travelling and balancing activities. In key stage 2, the pupils are asked to transfer themed skills and sequences from the floor to the benches in the corresponding units of work.

- Year R unit 1: Space, Listening Pose, Movement Patterns and Basic Shapes
- Year R unit 2: Basic Shapes and Balances: Stretch Shape, Tuck Shape and Star Shape
- Year R unit 3: Encouraging Safe Dismounts
- Year 1 and year 2 unit 5: Balances on Large and Small Body Parts Alongside Skipping
- Year 2 unit 6: Basic Shapes, Additional Rolling Techniques and Climbing
- Year 1 and year 2 unit 7: Jump, Land and Travel
- Year 3 unit 9: Symmetry and Group Balances
- Year 3 unit 10: Partner Up and Roll
- Year 4 unit 12: Building Boxes and Bridges
- Year 5 unit 13: Mirror, Match and Canon
- Year 5 unit 14: Push, Pull and Skip
- Year 6 unit 15: All Change
- Year 6 unit 16: Rock, Roll and Invert

The following six steps encourage the safe transportation of a gymnastics bench:

1. Stand pupils on either side of the bench, making either a V or a W, depending on how many pupils there are.
2. When lifting up or placing down the bench, lifters should not bend the body at the hips. Ensure that the body remains upright and the knees bend accordingly so that weight is taken in the legs and not the back.
3. Thumbs should be on the top of the bench when it is gripped.
4. Encourage all the pupils to face forward, looking and walking forward in the direction of travel.

5. The bench should be transported at approximately waist height.
6. Ensure a clear passage for the transport of the benches from the storage area to the activity station.

Platforms

Platforms allow pupils the opportunity to experience gymnastics skills such as balancing and jumping and landing with the added component of performing on varying levels and heights. In the foundation stage and key stage 1, platforms are used in the units for balance activities. In key stage 2, platforms are used in the units for balance and jump and land, and pupils are also asked to transfer themed skills and sequences from the floor to the platforms in the corresponding units of work.

- Year R unit 2: Basic Shapes and Balances: Stretch Shape, Tuck Shape and Star Shape
- Year 1 and year 2 unit 5: Balances on Large and Small Body Parts Alongside Skipping
- Year 2 unit 6: Basic Shapes, Additional Rolling Techniques and Climbing
- Year 3 unit 9: Symmetry and Group Balances
- Year 4 unit 11: Flighted Foot Patterns
- Year 5 unit 13: Mirror, Match and Canon
- Year 5 unit 14: Push, Pull and Skip
- Year 6 unit 16: Rock, Roll and Invert

The following six steps encourage the safe transport of a platform:

1. Position one or two pupils on each long side of a low platform; for a high platform, assign each pupil a platform leg.
2. Depending on its height, the platform can either be held on the top and supported with the thumbs on the top of the platform (same grip as used for the transport of mats, see figure 3.1d) or be supported by each pupil holding one of the platform legs with thumbs pointing upwards.
3. When lifting up or placing down the platform, ensure that the body remains upright and the knees bend accordingly. The body should not bend at the hips.
4. Encourage all the pupils to face forward, looking and walking forward in the direction of travel.
5. Where possible, depending on the height of the platform, the platform should be transported at approximately waist height.

6. Ensure a clear passage for the transport of the platform from the storage area to the activity station.

Wall Bars

Wall bars are largely underused in most primary schools. Many teachers worry about erecting the apparatus safely or lack creative ideas on exploration and experimentation for older pupils. The scheme of work on the DVD promotes the use of wall bars and provides many ideas for challenging activities for all ages.

The overall purpose of the wall bars is to encourage climbing and travelling skills. It is possible to form the five basic gymnastics shapes on the wall bars and to construct and build sequences involving both the climbing and travelling categories. Climbing and travelling activities do not require the use of mats under and around the wall bars. However, in unit 16 (Rock, Roll and Invert), an inversion activity using the wall bars is introduced. Because pupils are asked to turn upside down, the use of mats is required. In all units, it is not necessary for pupils to climb high to fulfil the task objectives; therefore it is reasonable to place markers on the wall bars to serve as height restrictions, especially for younger pupils.

In the foundation stage and key stage 1, pupils are asked to explore as many ways as possible to perform the basic gymnastics shapes on the wall bars; then they progress to constructing short sequences based on linking the shapes.

- Year R unit 3: Encouraging Safe Dismounts
- Year R unit 4: Early Rolling Techniques and Climbing
- Year 1 and year 2 unit 6: Basic Shapes, Additional Rolling Techniques and Climbing

In key stage 2, pupils are asked to transfer themed skills and sequences from the floor to the wall bars. Transfer of learnt gymnastics skills features in the following units of work:

- Year 3 unit 9: Symmetry and Group Balances
- Year 4 unit 12: Building Boxes and Bridges
- Year 5 unit 13: Mirror, Match and Canon
- Year 5 unit 14: Push, Pull and Skip
- Year 6 unit 16: Rock, Roll and Invert

Large apparatus such as wall bars should be set up according to the manufacturer's guidelines. Further checks should ensure the following:

- Floor grooves are clear of obstructions (dirt and dust) to ensure maximum depth is accessed by the bolts entering the floor fittings.
- All bolts are engaged and secured correctly in their floor and wall sockets.
- All wires are pulled taut and secured tightly to stabilise the apparatus.
- Any cord or ties are tied away and not left loose.
- All floor casters run smoothly.
- Wooden components are free from cracks or splinters.
- Painted components are well maintained with no evidence of flaking.

Whatever the function of gymnastics apparatus, teaching staff should ensure the following:

- Use approved apparatus that has been officially provided or Kitemarked (safety certified).
- Allow pupils to handle the apparatus during erecting and dismantling but ensure its placement and transportation are overseen by an adult. The equipment should be checked by an adult before the activity commences.
- Ensure the large apparatus is transported safely according to the guidelines offered for the large apparatus (mats, benches and platforms) at the beginning of this chapter.

Using Hand Apparatus

Following are the hand apparatus used throughout the units of work:

- Balls of all sizes
- Beanbags
- Hoops
- Ribbons, scarves or chiffons
- Skipping ropes

The use of hand apparatus introduces pupils to developing object control skills in a gymnastics environment. When working alongside a primary teacher and asking him or her to introduce a piece of hand apparatus in the lesson, I am often met with this reply: "But I thought we were doing gymnastics, not games!" And yes, we are. Hand apparatus allow pupils to take simple gymnastics skills and develop them into meaningful compositions through creative thinking.

Please note that hand apparatus should not be brought onto the large apparatus.

Balls

Most pupils love to play with balls, but when using balls in a gymnastics environment, you should take into consideration the level of control required for carrying out the activity safely. Balls are the most difficult piece of hand apparatus to control. Assess the possible risks involved if a pupil loses control of the ball. Gaining control of balls of all sizes encourages the development of eye–hand coordination and thus improves object control skills. When choosing a ball for the activity, consider the size of the ball in relation to the age and size of the pupil. Soft balls and sponge balls are easier to control than hard balls, which can roll and bounce away freely.

 Ball activities are featured in the following units of work on the DVD in the Scheme of Work folder:

- Year R unit 4: Early Rolling Techniques and Climbing
- KS2 unit 8: Mix 'n' Mingle Balances
- Year 4 unit 11: Flighted Foot Patterns
- Year 4 unit 12: Building Boxes and Bridges
- Year 5 unit 13: Mirror, Match and Canon
- Year 6 unit 16: Rock, Roll and Invert

Here are further ideas for developing basic ball control skills individually, with a partner or in a small group:

- Drop and catch the ball.
- Bounce the ball with one hand and repeat with other hand.

- Throw the ball into the air or against a wall and catch it.
- Roll the ball towards a target.
- Explore various ways to move the ball around the body.

Here are further ideas for implementing the ball into gymnastics skill tasks individually, with a partner or in a small group:

- Roll the ball around a partner, pair or small group performing basic gymnastics shapes (see figure 3.2).
- Roll a ball around a partner, pair or small group performing balances on large and small body parts.
- Explore various ways to move the ball over and around your body, focusing on control and creativity.
- Using movement patterns from the Creature Movements resource card, implement the ball into sequences.
- Using ideas from the Mix 'n' Mingle resource card, implement the ball into a sequence.
- Roll a ball to add variety and increase stretching techniques as described in unit 12, Building Boxes and Bridges.
- Using mirror, match and canon techniques in unit 13, implement the ball into composed sequences.
- Use a ball in movement patterns that demonstrate rotation around the vertical, horizontal and lateral axes.

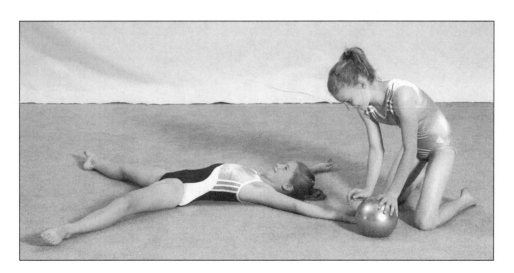

Figure 3.2   In pairs, roll a ball around a star shape.

Beanbags and Beanie Babies

Beanbags are ideal hand apparatus to use with younger pupils because they are easy to control and are particularly valuable when trying to encourage the gymnastics skill of balance. Beanbags can be used safely in areas of limited space. If Beanie Babies are available, younger pupils will enjoy the characters of these soft animals.

 Beanbag activities are featured in the following units of work on the DVD in the Scheme of Work folder:

- Year R unit 2: Basic Shapes and Balances: Stretch Shape, Tuck Shape and Star Shape
- Year 1 and year 2 unit 5: Balances on Large and Small Body Parts Alongside Skipping
- KS2 unit 8: Mix 'n' Mingle Balances
- Year 4 unit 11: Flighted Foot Patterns
- Year 5 unit 13: Mirror, Match and Canon

Here are further ideas for introducing basic beanbag control skills individually, with a partner or in a small group:

- Explore passing the beanbag by sliding, throwing or using hand-to-hand and hand-to-body-part techniques.
- Explore various ways to move the beanbag around the body, under the legs, over the shoulder, and so on.

- Practise controlled throwing and catching of the beanbag.

Here are further ideas for implementing beanbags into gymnastics skill tasks individually, with a partner or in a small group:

- Explore various ways to balance the beanbag around the body, focusing on control and creativity.
- Explore ways to balance the beanbag on various parts of the body when performing a basic gymnastics shape.
- Explore ways to balance the beanbag on various parts of the body when performing balances on large and small body parts (see figure 3.3).
- Balance the beanbag on the head and perform basic gymnastics shapes or balances on large and small body parts in a composed sequence.
- Using movement patterns from the Creature Movements resource card, implement the beanbag into sequences.
- Using ideas from the Mix 'n' Mingle resource card, implement the beanbag into a sequence.
- Using mirror, match and canon techniques in unit 13, implement the beanbag into composed sequences.
- Use a beanbag in movement patterns that demonstrate rotation around the vertical, horizontal and lateral axes.

Figure 3.3 In pairs, balancing beanbags on the body whilst performing a balance on a small body part.

Chiffons, Ribbons and Scarves

Activities with colourful, flowing materials engage pupils, are eye-catching and are easy to use. Always take into consideration the ages and sizes of the pupils when determining the length of the material: Smaller pupils may require shorter lengths of material. When using ribbons, ensure that adequate space is allocated to each pupil so that they can demonstrate full movement patterns.

 Chiffon, ribbon and scarf activities are featured in the following units of work on the DVD in the Scheme of Work folder:

- Year R unit 1: Space, Listening Pose, Movement Patterns and Basic Shapes
- Year 1 and year 2 unit 7: Jump, Land and Travel
- KS2 unit 8: Mix 'n' Mingle Balances
- Year 3 unit 9: Symmetry and Group Balances
- Year 5 unit 13: Mirror, Match and Canon
- Year 6 unit 16: Rock, Roll and Invert

Here are further ideas for basic ribbon control activities that focus on working individually, with a partner or in a small group:

- Explore ways to move the ribbon by using a variety of movement patterns (for example, circles, waves, zigzags, swirls, rainbows).

- Explore ways to move the ribbon by changing the size of the movement patterns (for example, large, medium and small).
- Explore ways to move the ribbon by changing the tempo of the movement patterns (for example, fast, medium and slow).
- Explore ways to move the ribbon by changing the level at which the movement pattern takes place (for example, from high to low and somewhere in between).
- Explore ways to move the ribbon around the body.
- Use the ribbon to demonstrate a variety of emotions through different movement patterns (see unit 9: Symmetry and Group Balances).

Here are further ideas for implementing ribbons into gymnastics skill tasks individually, with a partner or in a small group:

- Explore ways to move the ribbon when performing basic gymnastics shapes on various parts of the body (see figure 3.4).
- Explore ways to move the ribbon when performing balances on large and small body parts.
- Using movement patterns from the Creature Movements resource card, implement ribbon movement patterns into a sequence.
- Using ideas from the Mix 'n' Mingle resource card, implement ribbon movement patterns into a sequence.
- Using mirror, match and canon techniques in unit 13, implement ribbon movement patterns into composed sequences.
- Use ribbon movement patterns to demonstrate rotation around the vertical, horizontal and lateral axes.

Figure 3.4 Movement patterns with a ribbon whilst performing a tuck shape.

Hoops

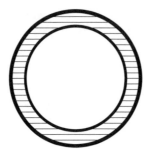

Hoops are great fun and have proven to be very versatile. You should take into consideration the size of the hoop in relation to the ages and sizes of the pupils: Small pupils may require smaller hoops. Hoops can also be noisy at times, especially if used in whole-class activities.

 Hoop activities are featured in the following units of work on the DVD in the Scheme of Work folder:

- Year R unit 3: Encouraging Safe Dismounts
- Year 1 and year 2 unit 6: Basic Shapes, Additional Rolling Techniques and Climbing
- KS2 unit 8: Mix 'n' Mingle Balances
- Year 4 unit 11: Flighted Foot Patterns
- Year 5 unit 13: Mirror, Match and Canon
- Year 6 unit 16: Rock, Roll and Invert

Here are further ideas for basic hoop control skills that focus on working individually, with a partner or in a small group:

- Explore passing the hoop by rolling or spinning or giving hand-to-hand or hand-to-body-part techniques.

- Explore various ways to move the hoop around the body.
- Explore skipping with the hoop forwards, backwards and sideways.
- Explore hula-hooping techniques.
- Explore balancing the hoop on various parts of the body.
- Explore rotating the hoop on different parts of the body (such as ankles, wrists, arms).
- Explore ways to travel into and out of the hoop with control.
- Explore ways to move through the hoop.

Here are further ideas for implementing hoops into gymnastics skill tasks individually, with a partner or in a small group:

- Explore various ways to move the hoop around your body, focusing on control and creativity.
- Explore ways to use the hoop when performing basic gymnastics shapes on various parts of the body.
- Explore ways to use the hoop when performing balances on large and small body parts.
- Using movement patterns from the Creature Movements resource card, implement the hoop into a sequence.
- Using ideas from the Mix 'n' Mingle resource card, implement a hoop into a sequence (see figure 3.5).

Figure 3.5 Performing basic gymnastics shapes with a hoop.

- Using mirror, match and canon techniques from unit 13, implement a hoop into composed sequences.
- Use a hoop in movement patterns that demonstrate rotation around the vertical, horizontal and lateral axes.

Skipping Ropes

Skipping is a fabulous way to have fun and improve fitness without really knowing it. Skipping with a rope is primarily thought of as a high-impact activity that complements the development of locomotor skills, but a skipping rope can also be used in low-impact activities; this ensures that activities with a skipping rope are inclusive and attainable to all pupils. Physiologically, high-impact skipping develops bone density in young children, thus increasing the long-term strength of the weight-bearing bones. It also improves cardiorespiratory fitness and muscular endurance. Once pupils learn the basic skipping skill, you can extend the activity by creatively designing various skipping steps and composing short sequences. Use of a skipping rope as a low-impact activity involves swinging movement patterns with the rope and requires pupils to be creative when composing sequences. The rope should be folded so that it is about 30 centimetres long, and a generous space should be allocated to each pupil when performing low-impact rope tasks. Skipping activities can be social actions that promote the benefits of teamwork. Remember to practice new skills without a rope first.

Skipping ropes made of cotton material are by far the best equipment to use because they maintain their shape during storage, they move easily through the air without distortion, and they cause little or no pain when coming into contact with the body. Other manufactured plastic-like ropes lose their shape, are too light to travel through the air without distortion, and sting if they come into contact with the body.

Progressions for Learning to Skip

Skipping with a rope consists of coordinating two very different actions: jumping over an obstacle (the rope) and rotating a length of material (the rope) 360 degrees continuously. The skills can

be broken down into easy steps for beginners to learn. Instruct the pupils to do the following:

1. Hold the rope in the hands (ensuring that it is of a suitable length for the size of the body) with the rope still on the floor in front of you.
2. Jump or step over the rope, encouraging the rope not to move.
3. Put the hands next to the shoulders and throw the rope by extending the arms upwards and forwards. The rope will rotate and lift overhead to land on the floor in front of the feet. This is difficult, and assistance might be required.
4. Repeat the process.

Rope activities are featured in the following units of work on the DVD in the Scheme of Work folder:

- Year R unit 3: Encouraging Safe Dismounts
- Year 1 and year 2 unit 5: Balances on Large and Small Body Parts Alongside Skipping (high- and low-impact rope activities)
- Year 2 unit 7: Jump, Land and Travel
- Year 3 unit 10: Partner Up and Roll (low-impact rope activities)
- Year 4 unit 11: Flighted Foot Patterns
- Year 5 unit 13: Mirror, Match and Canon
- Year 5 unit 14: Push, Pull and Skip
- Year 6 unit 15: All Change
- Year 6 unit 16: Rock, Roll and Invert

Here are further ideas for basic object control skills with a skipping rope that focus on working individually, with a partner or in a small group:

- **Low impact.** Explore ways to move the rope by using a variety of swinging movement patterns involving a change in direction.
- **Low impact.** Explore ways to move the rope by changing the level at which the movement pattern takes place (for example, from high to low and somewhere in between).
- **Low impact.** Explore ways to move the rope around, under and over the body.
- **High impact.** Explore using different foot patterns when passing over the rope (for example, jumping, hopping, jumping jacks, flick kicks, scissor steps, twister jumps).

- **High impact.** Challenge your stamina and explore skipping for various lengths of time, such as 2 minutes.
- **High impact.** Challenge your speed and challenge how many skips you can perform in a set time, such as 20 seconds.
- **High impact.** Explore skipping with a partner.
- **High impact.** Explore skipping in small groups.
- **Low and high impact.** Explore ways to travel over and under a rope.
- **Low and high impact.** Explore ways to combine low-impact rope-swinging movements with high-impact skipping steps.

Here are further ideas for implementing skipping ropes into gymnastics skill tasks individually, with a partner or in a small group:

- Explore ways to move the rope when performing basic gymnastics shapes on various parts of the body (see figure 3.6a).
- Explore ways to move the rope when performing balances on large and small body parts.
- Using movement patterns from the Creature Movements resource card, implement rope movement patterns and skipping techniques into a sequence.
- Using ideas from the Mix 'n' Mingle resource card, implement rope movement patterns or skipping techniques into a sequence.
- Using mirror, match and canon techniques in unit 13, implement rope movement patterns or skipping techniques into composed sequences.

- Use rope movement patterns and skipping techniques to demonstrate rotation around the vertical, horizontal and lateral axes (see figure 3.6b).

Impermissible Apparatus for Primary Schools

Certain items of gymnastics equipment are not permitted for use in primary schools. Examples are rebound jumping equipment such as springboards and trampettes, trampolines and landing modules (perhaps better known as crash mats). The use of these pieces of gymnastics equipment requires specialised knowledge and training before being included as a teaching aid in a primary curriculum gymnastics lesson. The national governing body (NGB) for gymnastics in each country will be able to answer any questions regarding teaching awards or qualifications required for implementing the use of gymnastics-specific equipment in primary gymnastics.

Now that you have learnt about using the large apparatus and hand apparatus available in your own school, the chapters in part II present the teaching directives that will enable you to instruct your pupils in the basic gymnastics skills and initiate the activities involving the apparatus.

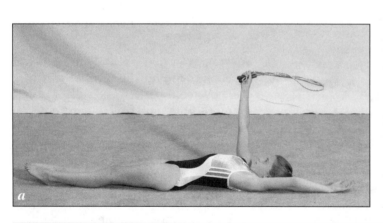

Figure 3.6 (a) Low impact activity with skipping rope, swinging the rope whist performing a stretch shape; (b) high impact activity with skipping rope—jumping over the rope during a skipping activity.

Attainment and Assessment

Assessing pupils' progress allows you to ascertain where your pupils are, where they need to be and how they are going to get where they need to be with regard to the attainment guides in the foundation stage scale points and the key stage 1 and key stage 2 level descriptors. Assessment is dependent on the effectiveness of the planning of lessons and the delivery of the instruction. If there are clear long-term, medium-term and short-term learning objectives as defined in chapter 2, Ensuring Effective Delivery of Gymnastics in Primary Education, you already will have clearly defined expectations of your pupils. On the DVD, each unit of work contains specific learning objectives in the form of learning intentions and learning outcomes (remember that you may select your own rather than follow the ones chosen), and pupils are provided with progressions of learning and a variety of opportunities established through diverse tasks to demonstrate what they have learnt, enabling you as a teacher to gather evidence from which

to make assessments on your pupils' attainment regarding the scale points and level descriptors outlined as seen in table 4.1. Assessing pupils will allow you to track their progress over time, thus promoting teaching that is matched to pupils' needs and meets the national standards. In all cases, you will need to consider the evidence before making a judgement.

Foundation Stage Profile for Assessment

Notes taken from Qualifications and Curriculum Authority (2007). *Early Years Foundation Stage Profile Handbook 2008.* London: Department for Children, Schools and Families (DCSF).

When pupils enter primary education in reception, they each arrive with an ongoing early years "learning journey," which may be in the form of a scrap book containing data that can be used for a variety of purposes but will essentially contain information and evidence regarding their

Table 4.1 Physical Development: Foundation Stage Profile Assessment Scale Points

SP1 Moves spontaneously, showing some control and coordination.	SP2 Moves with confidence in a variety of ways, showing some awareness of space.		SP3 Usually shows appropriate control in large and small scale movements.	
SP4 Moves with confidence and imagination and in safety. Travels around, under, over and through balancing and climbing equipment. Shows awareness of space, of self and of others.	SP5 Demonstrates fine motor control and coordination.	SP6 Uses small and large equipment, showing a range of basic skills.	SP7 Handles tools, objects and malleable materials safely and with basic control.	SP8 Recognises the importance of keeping healthy and those things that contribute to this. Recognises the changes that happen to her/his body when s/he is active.
SP9 Repeats, links and adapts simple movements, sometimes commenting on her or his work. Demonstrates coordination and control in large and small movements and in using a range of tools and equipment.				

Notes taken from the National Assessment Agency, Quality Assurance of Early Years Foundation Stage Profile Data, Sept 2008.

attainment levels in each area of learning, including physical development. The early learning goals for physical development represent the expected level of attainment to be achieved by the end of a pupil's reception year in the foundation stage. The scale points are organised into three levels, and most children will already be working towards achieving certain scale points upon entry to primary education.

Information regarding pupils' physical development should be acquired over time and through a variety of activities such as

- physical tasks in a range of environments, including individual learning, working with a partner and group tasks;
- classroom-based tasks such as information and communication technology assignments; and
- in discussion opportunities through question-and-answer dialogue.

Judgements are based on observational evidence; therefore, it is expected that all adults who interact with pupils will contribute to the process and that account will also be taken of information provided by parents. Evidence is attained from teachers' knowledge of the pupil and observation of the pupil's activities and actions. You should regularly check and amend judgements, and you might find the following questions useful when moderating the evidence:

- Are judgements consistent and accurate?
- Has a range of evidence (predominantly from observation of child-initiated activities) been used to support judgements?
- Is evidence supporting a pupil's attainment of a particular scale point appropriate?
- How does the evidence match scale point criteria?
- Are scale points interrogated closely to ensure that all elements are actually achieved?

Evidence can be supported by photos, which will also aid consistency when making judgements. Remember that each pupil will achieve and progress at a different pace depending on his or her starting point and other factors, including opportunity.

Scale points 1 to 9 are presented in an approximate order of difficulty. It is important to take into account that pupils are expected to complete scale points 1 to 3 (which describe a pupil who is still progressing towards the achievements) securing a baseline scale point score of 3 before moving on to achieving scale points 4 to 8. Scale points 4 to 8 are not hierarchical and must not be assessed or completed in numerical order. For each scale point achieved, 1 is added to the base score of 3. For example, if a pupil attained scale points 4 and 6, then a 2 would be added to the base score to create a total of 5. Scale point 9 is achievable only through the achievement of skills in scale points 1 to 8 and indicates that a pupil is working consistently beyond the level of the early learning goals.

Key Stage 1 and Key Stage 2 Physical Education Attainment Targets: Level Descriptions 1 to 5

The attainment targets in physical education set out the knowledge, skills and understanding that pupils are expected to have by the end of key stage 1 and key stage 2. The level descriptors used in assessing a pupil's understanding of the tasks performed can also support planning and teaching. The level descriptors show progression in the four aspects of learning,

1. Acquiring and developing skills
2. Selecting and applying skills, tactics and compositional ideas
3. Evaluating and improving performance
4. Knowledge and understanding of fitness and health

In key stage 1 the majority of pupils are expected to work at levels 1 to 3, and level 2 is the national expectation for a year 2 pupil at the end of key stage 1. In key stage 2 the majority of pupils are expected to work at levels 3 to 5, and level 4 is the national expectation for a year 6 pupil at the end of key stage 2. The additional grading of an *a*, *b* or *c* at each level 1, 2, 3, 4, or 5 allows you to demonstrate whether a pupil has just reached this level of assessment and graded a *c*, is capably working at this level and graded a *b* or is more than competently working at this level and graded an *a*. See table 4.2 for more details.

Guidelines for Assessing Gymnastics Performances in Key Stage 1 and Key Stage 2

The learning objectives provided in each unit of work in the scheme of work on the DVD can be used to evaluate the effectiveness of learn-

Table 4.2   KS1 and KS2 Level Descriptors

Level	Acquiring and developing skills	Selecting and applying skills, tactics and compositional ideas	Evaluating and improving performance	Knowledge and understanding of fitness and health
1 c b a	Copy, repeat and explore simple skills and actions with basic control and coordination.	Start to link these skills and actions in ways that suit the activity.	Describe and comment on own and others' actions.	Talk about how to exercise safely and how the body feels during an activity.
2 c b a	Explore simple skills. Copy, remember, repeat and explore simple actions with control and coordination.	Vary skills, actions and ideas and link these in ways that suit the activities. Begin to understand simple tactics and compositional ideas.	Talk about differences between own and others' performance and suggest improvements.	Understand how to exercise safely and describe how the body feels during various activities.
Level 2b/a is the national expectation for a year 2 pupil (end of KS1).				
3 c b a	Use skills with coordination and control.	Select actions and ideas appropriately, applying them. Show an understanding of tactics and basic compositional ideas.	See how their work is similar to or different to others' work, and use this understanding to improve own performance.	Give reasons why warming up before an activity is important and why physical activity is important for health.
4 c b a	Link skills, techniques and ideas. Performance shows precision, control and fluency.	Link skills and apply them accurately and appropriately whilst understanding tactics and composition.	Compare and comment on skills, techniques and ideas used in own and others' work, and use this understanding to improve performance.	Explain and apply safety principles in preparing for exercise. Describe what effects exercise has on the body and how it is valuable to fitness and health.
Level 4b/a is the national expectation for a year 6 pupil (end of KS2).				
5 c b a	Combine skills, techniques and ideas consistently, showing precision, control and fluency.	Select and apply skills accurately and appropriately. When performing, draw on knowledge about strategy, tactics and composition.	Analyse and comment on skills and techniques and how these are applied in own and others' work. Modify and refine skills and techniques to improve performance.	Explain how the body reacts during different types of exercise. Warm up and cool down in ways that suit the activity. Explain why regular, safe exercise is good for fitness and health.

Based on http://curriculum.qcda.gov.uk/key-stages-1-and-2/subjects/physical-education/attainmenttarget/index.aspx.

ing in gymnastics, and the expectations of the tasks for most pupils can be used in assessing attainment targets and plotting progression through key stage 1 and key stage 2 gymnastics. Assessments should be based on pupils' overall performance and should take into account both the strengths and weaknesses of performances. Judgements should be made from several varied performances and recorded consistently over time.

Information regarding pupils' attainment should be acquired over time and through a variety of activities such as,

- physical tasks in a range of environments, including individual learning, working with a partner and group tasks;
- classroom based tasks such as information and communication technology assignments and

- in discussion opportunities through question and answer dialogue.

A single piece of work will therefore not cover all the expectations set out in a level descriptor, and you should take into account strengths and weaknesses in pupils' performances across a range of contexts over a period of time.

Judgements will be based on the degree to which each pupil meets the knowledge, skills and understanding of criteria as described under the four aspects of learning and demonstrated across a range of gymnastics activities. The four aspects of learning do not have to be assessed separately, although depending on the task, this may be a more appropriate approach. You will need to consider how far a pupil is able to adapt his or her knowledge and skills and apply them for various purposes in a range of gymnastics activities with a view to altering the outcome and performance design.

You will need to make judgements when pupils are evaluating and improving performances to ensure that they are making the connections between developing skills with technical accuracy, selecting and applying skills and implementing tactics and compositional ideas to enhance performance. *Complete Guide to Primary Gymnastics* encourages pupils to evaluate their own and others' performances through the "stars and wishes" approach. Pupils are asked to describe two stars, which are factors that they liked about the performance, and to choose one wish, which is a piece of constructive criticism designed to improve a performance. Refer to chapter 2 in the book for more information regarding evaluation and improvement techniques.

Pupils should be given opportunities to demonstrate attainment. The gymnastics tasks and activities chosen should reflect pupils' age and ability. Pupils will need to use a range of communication and discussion techniques to demonstrate what they know; this can be demonstrated through the information and communication technology tasks in each unit of work, and opportunities should exist for pupils to show what they know and understand (through question-and-answer sessions and through the planning of activities, such as warming up and cooling down).

The correct use of vocabulary and the ability to verbalise their own and others' performances through observation techniques and sound technical understanding will demonstrate a good understanding of the tasks involved. In the preparation and implementation of the gymnastics units of work, it is necessary to provide opportunities for pupils to display their achievements both in practical gymnastics activities and through theory-based classroom approaches. Examples may include planning a sequence demonstrated through the use of words and drawings or organising gymnastics competitions and festivals. Pupils may also benefit from using video to analyse performance and select targets for improvements. (Decisions about collecting information, its purpose and how it should be used are matters for teachers working within an agreed school policy.) Judging these and other performances will require the use of evaluation and improvement strategies explained in chapter 2. Leading and organising others in practices and performances will provide pupils with the opportunity to demonstrate their knowledge, skills and understanding. Attainment and assessment of pupils' performances may also take place in out-of-school learning environments, such as gymnastics clubs and other organised physical activity programmes.

Features of Progressions in Gymnastics Based on the Scheme of Work on the DVD

In the foundation stage, pupils are expected to explore basic gymnastics shapes, actions and movement patterns to develop control, coordination and consistency in their gymnastics. Pupils are also expected to extend their knowledge of language to enable them to recognise and act on gymnastics-specific vocabulary used in the introduction of basic gymnastics shapes and actions. Pupils are introduced to the large apparatus and hand apparatus.

- In key stage 1 pupils acquire and develop skills building on their knowledge of basic gymnastics shapes, actions and movement patterns. Gymnastics-specific skills are progressed through the gymnastics formula: shape + action = gymnastics skills.

- In key stage 1 pupils are expected to select and apply learnt gymnastics skills and actions and to perform them in different contexts using the large apparatus and hand apparatus. Pupils are also expected to select and apply gymnastics-specific skills, actions and movement patterns to compose simple sequences.

- In key stage 1 pupils are encouraged to evaluate and improve their own and others' performances by accurately describing what they observe and to verbalise gymnastics skills using their knowledge of basic gymnastics shapes and actions. Pupils are asked through question-and-answer dialogue to explain health and safety points with regards to gymnastics-specific skill acquisition and the use of apparatus.

- In key stage 1 a pupil's understanding and knowledge of fitness and health will focus on recognising that physical activity causes physiological changes to the body. Pupils should be able to identify the difference between the bones, muscles and joints of the body and understand that physical activity is good for health.

- In key stage 2 pupils acquire and develop skills displaying more control, technical accuracy and consistency. Pupils will show an improved level of confidence allowing them to develop artistically and demonstrate a variety of entrances and exits from skills. Pupils develop skills with a partner based on their knowledge of basic gymnastics shapes and their understanding of the action of balance to attain a repertoire of paired balances. Pupils are encouraged to work in small groups to develop teamwork techniques and to challenge problem-solving tasks.

- In key stage 2 pupils select and apply skills based on themed ideas applying tactics and compositional ideas. Pupils will dem-onstrate complex sequences individually, in pairs or in small groups performing gymnastics-specific skills and movement patterns consistent with the basic criteria of the chosen theme displaying creativity and flair.

- In key stage 2 pupils' evaluation techniques should include an understanding of technical knowledge to aid improvement in their own and others' performances. Pupils should also be able to form evaluations of their own and others' performances based on their knowledge of good posture and presentation skills and be able to provide constructive criticism to enable improvement to progress.

- In key stage 2 a pupil's understanding and knowledge of fitness and health will demonstrate an understanding of how and why physical activity causes changes to the body. Pupils should demonstrate a basic knowledge of the bones, muscles and joints of the body and be able to explain the purpose of each. Pupils should understand and be able to explain why warming up and cooling down are important when under-taking physical activity. Pupils should be able to recognise the long-term benefits of participating in physical activity.

PART

II

Gymnastics Warm-Up, Cool-Down, Techniques and Games

Part II focuses on what to include and how to instruct gymnastics-specific skills, those key elements that will ensure your lesson is uniquely gymnastics based. You begin in chapter 5 with learning why pupils need to prepare for and recover from physical activity.

Chapters 6 and 7 introduce the gymnastics shapes used in this resource that form the foundations of all gymnastics-specific skill acquisition. Chapter 6 introduces the basic gymnastics shapes that you will use throughout your entire gymnastics curriculum. You will learn the vocabulary and properties of the shapes, which underpin the development of all skills throughout the resource. Basic gymnastics shapes progress to the more challenging postural shapes in chapter 7, where improvement in posture and core stability are emphasised. Each shape is introduced by reviewing the properties of the shape. Every gymnastics shape has a teaching points section, which provides teachers with key technical advice on how to perform the shapes correctly. This section is highlighted with a star in text as well as in the pictorial resources on the DVD. This is knowledge that should be shared with the pupils to enhance their understanding and ensure technical accuracy when they attempt to perform the shapes. All of this information is followed by an early attempts section that outlines the most frequently appearing technical errors and provides teachers with information on how to improve the appearance of the gymnastics shape as well as a set of images and where on the DVD the shape's pictorial resource can be located. The gymnastics-specific skills linked to each shape are listed alongside its location on the DVD. Mastering the basic gymnastics shapes and postural shapes will provide pupils with the prerequisite skills that will enable them to acquire gymnastics-specific skills such as rolls, inversions and paired balances, which are covered in the next three chapters.

Chapter 8 presents an extensive range of simple gymnastics rolls to teach your pupils and also includes instruction for teaching the forward roll. Chapter 9 is all about turning upside down and includes instruction for teaching some of the more difficult gymnastics skills, such as the bridge, handstand and cartwheel. Chapter 10 covers partner work, which provides your pupils with progressive skills and challenging movements. In these chapters the properties of each gymnastics-specific skill are outlined first explaining the gymnastics shape and action required to perform the skill. Every gymnastics-specific skill has a teaching points section, which provides teachers with key technical advice on how to perform the skill correctly. This section is highlighted with a star in text as well as in the pictorial resources on the DVD. This is knowledge that should be shared with the pupils to enhance their understanding and ensure technical accuracy when they attempt to perform the skill. Pictures of the gymnastics-specific skill provide a visual element invaluable for anyone who is unfamiliar with the technical clarity of gymnastics skills. There is also an early attempts section that outlines the most frequently appearing technical errors and provides teachers with information to improve the appearance of the gymnastics-specific skill. The gymnastics-specific skills are noted alongside where the skills can be found in units of work in the Scheme of Work folder on the DVD.

Chapter 11 is all about fun and games. It describes the themed games used in this teaching resource, which are variations of games used in other areas of physical activity. What makes the themed games unique is that they are specific to gymnastics and are relevant to the lessons.

Preparing For and Recovering From Physical Activity

I n your gymnastics lessons, it is necessary to plan a beginning (the warm-up) and an ending (the cool-down) to allow your pupils the opportunity to prepare for physical activity and then recover from physical activity before leaving the gymnastics lesson. It's ideal for the preparation and recovery to include a physically active component for the body and a focusing component for the mind. The latter is often overlooked, but in my classes it is one of my primary concerns. Think of the mental preparation in the warm-up and its conclusion in the cool-down as akin to the beginning and ending of a story. If you miss the beginning, it can be difficult to understand the middle; if you miss the ending, you might not fully understand what has happened. Effective physical activity requires cognitive understanding, and the preparation for and recovery from activities offer the ideal opportunity for you to impart relevant knowledge. You will notice that in all the units of work on the DVD, the warm-up activities and cool-down activities in the themed games and physical literacy ideas are very specific to the focus of the lesson, and most contain relevant discussion points that you can share with your pupils.

Preparing For Physical Activity: The Warm-Up

The warm-up prepares the body and mind for physical activity, ensures an acceptable level of safety and encourages pupils to think about how their bodies work and how their own thought processes control their actions. In regard to gymnastics, the warm-up should be directly related to the activities and content of the gymnastics unit to be covered during the lesson.

The warm-up should contain four components:

1. Pulse raiser
2. Mobility
3. Flexibility
4. Mental preparation

Warm-Up Focus for Foundation Stage and Key Stage 1

The warm-up for pupils in the foundation stage and key stage 1 should focus on a controlled pulse raiser, mobility exercises and mental preparation. It should include activities that are directly related to the unit of work the pupils are covering. The themed warm-up games brought into play in the early stages are good fun and promote the learning of the basic gymnastics shapes. Road Traffic Signs, Washing the Clothes, and Gymnastics Bean games are based on everyday concepts familiar to most young pupils. Static stretching exercises for individual muscle groups are difficult for younger pupils, but whole-body stretches based on the stretch, star and tuck shapes may be safely included.

Warm-Up Focus for Key Stage 2

The warm-up for pupils in key stage 2 should include a controlled pulse raiser, mobility, stretching exercises and mental preparation. It should include activities that are directly related to the unit of work they are covering. The themed game Creature Movements is a fun activity to use as a pulse raiser because it is creative, it encourages the development and understanding of varied movement patterns and it promotes whole-body activities. Physical literacy ideas featured in chapter 11 also provide challenging activities ideal for use as pulse raisers.

Stretching exercises that focus on large muscle groups should be included. In lower key stage 2, static stretching is advised. In upper key stage 2, it may be possible to introduce controlled dynamic stretching techniques.

Pulse Raisers

A pulse raiser exercise raises body temperature. The increased rate of respiration and blood circulation enables an increased uptake of oxygen and glucose to the muscles and organs, which improves the rate of waste removal so that the muscles can function more effectively.

Chapter 11, Themed Games, contains many pulse raiser activities. The games introduce basic and postural gymnastics shapes, and the themes are based on everyday concepts familiar to most young pupils. The physical literacy ideas outlined in chapter 11 can also be used as pulse raisers.

 In the Pictorial Resources folder, refer to the files in the Themed Games folder.

In the Pictorial Resources folder, refer to the Mix 'n' Mingle Balances file in the Balance Combinations folder.

Mobility Exercises

Mobility is a controlled movement of joints through their normal range. Mobility exercises ensure that the joints of the body are lubricated and continue to move freely. All movement occurs at the joints where the bones and muscles meet. Joints are stabilised by ligaments joining bone to bone and tendons joining muscle to bone.

There are several types of joints in the body, all with different structures and functions. Pupils in key stage 2 should be familiar with the following two joints and their functional capabilities. The actions and roles of these joints should be highlighted in the warm-up.

- Ball-and-socket joints: The bones of the hip joint are the femur and pelvis, and the bones of the shoulder joint consist of the humerus and scapula. These joints allow 360-degree rotational movement.
- Hinge joints: The bones of the elbow joint are the humerus, radius and ulna; the bones of the knee joint are the femur, tibia and fibula. These joints allow an open-and-close movement from 0 to 180 degrees.

The role of the skeleton in physical activity is to provide a framework on which to attach muscles that contract and relax to enable movement. The skeleton also gives the body its shape and protects the vital organs of the brain, spinal cord, heart and lungs.

Following are several mobility exercises for all ages:

NECK

- Nod gently.
- Turn gently side to side.

SHOULDERS

- Shrug shoulders.
- Rotate shoulders.
- Circle arms forwards, backwards and alternating directions (one arm in each direction).

ELBOWS

- Bend elbows, lifting hands to shoulders.
- Turn lower arm, rotating from elbow with palms down, then palms up.

WRISTS

- Circle hands.
- Link fingers and move hands and arms in a wavy motion.

FINGERS AND THUMBS

- Wiggle fingers.
- Circle thumbs.
- Flex and extend fingers and thumbs.

HIPS

Circle hips in both directions.

KNEES

- Bend and lift knee forwards to horizontal (involves hip mobility as well).
- Lift foot to buttocks, bending at knee.
- Attempt lifting knee or foot to opposite hand (cross-lateral development).

ANKLES

Do heel and toe tapping variations.

TOES

Scrunch up toes.

 In the Dartfish Mediabooks folder, refer to the Mobility of Joints mediabook in the Warming Up mediabook folder for all the proper techniques for mobility exercises.

Stretching Exercises

Stretching maintains the pliability of large muscles and joints. As the body grows and ages, the muscles tend to lose flexibility. Regular stretching helps to minimize loss of flexibility in an aging body. Stretching exercises should take place when the body is warm because the muscles will be more pliable; therefore after a pulse raiser and during the cool-down are ideal times for stretching. Stretching prepares the muscles for an increased physical demand and helps to prevent muscular injuries, such as pulls or strains. Stretching after physical activity aids in the recovery of the muscles. Stretching exercises in the warm-up should be held for 6 to 10 seconds; stretching exercises in the cool-down (when the muscles are generally warmer and more pliable) can be held for longer, perhaps 15 to 20 seconds.

Pupils should ease their bodies into a stretch exercise to the point where the muscle feels a little uncomfortable but not painful. Pupils should never strain or bounce because that can damage the joints and muscles. Pupils should be able to refer to the large muscles they are stretching by name, such as the quadriceps, hamstrings and triceps. Remember to include stretching exercises at the beginning and at the end of the gymnastics lesson.

Static Stretching Exercises

Static stretching involves controlled extension of the large muscle groups whilst maintaining a stable position. Most key stage 2 pupils will be able to approach this type of stretching in a safe and effective manner. Static stretches should involve the following large muscle groups:

RHOMBOIDS AND TRAPEZIUS

- The rhomboid and trapezius muscles are across the upper back.
- Join hands in front of the body and push palms forwards, straightening the arms and lowering the head (see figure 5.1).

Figure 5.1 Stretching the rhomboids and trapezius muscles across the upper back.

TRICEPS

- The triceps muscle is at the back of the upper arm.
- Lift one arm to horizontal and bend at elbow so hand rests on opposite shoulder.
- Place palm of opposite hand at the back of the bent elbow and gently push (see figure 5.2).

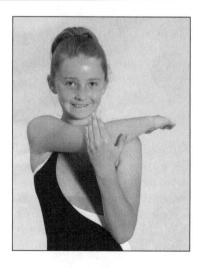

Figure 5.2 Stretching the triceps muscle at the back of the upper arm.

DELTOIDS

- The deltoid muscles are at the front of the shoulders.
- Link hands together behind back and gently lift arms upwards. Body remains upright (see figure 5.3).

Figure 5.3 Stretching the deltoids muscles at front of the shoulders.

OBLIQUES

- The obliques are the muscles on the sides of the waist.
- Stand with the feet apart and knees soft. Place hands on hips.
- Gently turn the upper body from side to side (see figure 5.4).

Figure 5.4 Stretching the oblique muscles on the sides of the waist.

SERRATUS

- The serratus muscles are along the sides of the upper body.
- Stand with the feet apart and knees soft. Place both hands on the hips or place one hand on the hip and extend the other hand vertically into the air.
- Gently extend and lean the upper body over sideways, maintaining support of the upper body from the hand on the hip (see figure 5.5).

Figure 5.5 Stretching the serratus muscles along the sides of the upper body.

QUADRICEPS

- The quadriceps (or quad) muscles are at the front of the upper legs.
- Stand on one leg (support may be required) and bend opposite leg. Extend foot to buttock and hold the ankle.
- Try to keep the angle at the hip open, encouraging the knees to stay together or for the knee of the bent leg to be behind the knee of the supporting leg (see figure 5.6).

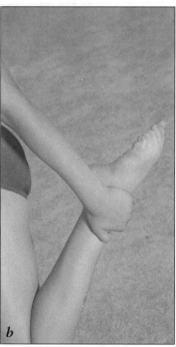

Figure 5.6 *(a)* Stretching the quadriceps at the front of the upper leg; *(b)* correct hold on ankle for performing quadriceps stretch.

a

b

HAMSTRINGS

- The hamstrings are the muscles at the back of the upper legs.
- Place one foot in front of the other and pretend to sit down slightly by bending the back leg.
- Support the upper body by placing the hands on the upper leg, keeping the back flat and the head looking forwards (see figure 5.7a).
- An alternative hamstring stretch would be to adopt the seated pike shape and walk the hands forwards, keeping the legs straight, the back flat and the head looking forwards (see figure 5.7b).

Figure 5.7 *(a)* Stretching the hamstrings at the back of the upper legs; *(b)* stretching the hamstrings in a seated pike stretch.

ADDUCTORS

- The adductor muscles are on the inside of the upper leg.
- Adopt the straddle shape and walk the hands forwards. Keep the legs wide and straight with the knees pointing upwards, the back flat and the head looking forwards (see figure 5.8).

Figure 5.8 Stretching the adductors *(a)* on the inside of the upper leg; *(b)* stretching to the right side.

CALVES

- The calves are the muscles at the back of the lower legs.
- Place one foot in front of the other with both feet pointing forwards.
- Gently bend the front knee whilst pressing the heel of the back foot into the floor (see figure 5.9).

 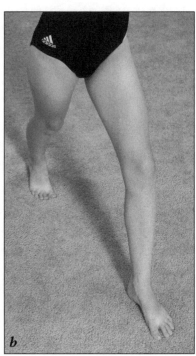

Figure 5.9 (a) Stretching the calf muscles; (b) correct foot placement for stretching the calf muscles.

 In the Pictorial Resources folder, refer to the Static Stretches file.

Dynamic Stretching Exercises

Dynamic stretching involves controlled extension of the large muscle groups whilst in motion. Most upper key stage 2 pupils will be able to do this type of stretching in an acceptably safe and effective manner. Dynamic stretches can include the following exercises:

HEEL RAISE

- This exercise stretches and builds the calf muscles and promotes a sense of balance.
- Walk by stepping onto the heel first and then rising onto the toes.

ROTATOR

- This exercise mobilises and stretches the groin area.
- Walk by lifting knee to horizontal and rotating outwards.

TWISTER

- This exercise mobilises and stretches the oblique muscles of the waist area. It also mobilises and stretches the hip joint if the knee crosses the central line of the body.
- Walk by lifting knee to opposite elbow and twisting the body around the waist (ensure knee lifts to elbow action; do not drop elbow to knee).

BUTTOCKS KICKER

- This exercise stretches quadriceps muscles.
- Gently jog, placing hands on the buttocks and kick feet upwards towards hands whilst knees point downwards.

GOOSE WALK

- This exercise stretches the hamstring muscles.
- Walk by lifting knee to horizontal and slowly extend the leg forwards. Increase the stretch by flexing the foot as well.

COFFEE GRINDER

- This exercise mobilises the shoulders.
- Hold hands with a partner. Both partners turn to pass under hands; arms complete a full turn. Repeat in opposite direction.

 In the Dartfish Mediabooks folder, refer to the heel raise, rotator, twister, buttocks kicker, goose walk and coffee grinder clips in the Dynamic Stretching mediabook in the Warming Up mediabook folder.

Mental Preparation

Mental preparation focuses the mind and prepares participants psychologically for physical activity. Mental preparation in the warm-up is the most important factor in ensuring that pupils are ready to receive instructions and process the information accurately. The body is controlled by the brain, which is responsible for all decisions regarding physical movements. Mental preparation ensures that pupils are responsible and accountable for their actions, which in turn will ensure improved body management and control.

Mental preparation activities are simple to carry out and can take the form of asking pupils to follow a basic set of instructions (refer to the physical literacy ideas in chapter 11), to copy a series of actions (mirroring) or simply to encourage a discussion about the gymnastics lesson. Discussion regarding the content of the lesson is very important, and pupils will learn more efficiently if they understand the purpose of the skills and tasks they perform. The dialogue technique works equally well at the beginning and at the end of a lesson.

Dos and Don'ts in the Warm-Up

- ✓ **Do** encourage a controlled and challenging pulse raiser.
- ⊘ **Don't** allow an uncontrolled pulse raiser with too much noise (pulse raising activities can excite pupils).

 ✅ **Do** ensure the pulse raiser is a mix of high- and low-impact activities.

 ⊘ **Don't** allow all high-impact and vigorous activities in the pulse raiser.

 ✅ **Do** watch for signs of fatigue.

 ⊘ **Don't** exhaust pupils; it will seriously affect their concentration and safety throughout the remainder of the lesson.

 ✅ **Do** keep abreast of safety guidelines on exercises.

 ⊘ **Don't** assume current research into safe exercises is conclusive.

 ✅ **Do** approach stretches in a controlled manner.

 ⊘ **Don't** approach stretches in an uncontrolled manner, which can result in quick and jerky actions.

 ✅ **Do** encourage good body posture throughout.

 ⊘ **Don't** allow sloppiness in body posture.

 ✅ **Do** include activities relevant to the focus of the lesson.

 ⊘ **Don't** include activities that are not relevant to the main focus of the lesson.

 ✅ **Do** focus on mobilisation and stretching exercises that are relevant to the main activity of the lesson (such as a jump and land activity and stretching the large muscles in legs).

 ⊘ **Don't** focus mobilisation and stretching exercises that are not relevant to the main activity (such as mobilising the wrists for a jump and land activity).

 ✅ **Do** involve and include all the pupils by using simple, easy-to-organise activities.

 ⊘ **Don't** choose complicated activities that some pupils might find difficult to understand.

Following are long-term benefits of performing an effective warm-up:

- Reduces risk of injury
- Improves fitness levels
- Improves mobility and flexibility
- Adds fun and variety

Recovering From Physical Activity: The Cool-Down

The cool-down returns the body to its resting status by slowing down the activity in a controlled manner. The cool-down is an important part of the end of the lesson and helps pupils to prepare their bodies to stop being physically active. The cool-down is particularly significant for young pupils, who often become excitable during physical activity and need calming before returning to classroom-based activities.

The cool-down allows the body temperature to cool naturally, the rate of respiration to return to normal, and the blood circulation to return to normal, lowering blood pressure. Activities in the cool-down should include stretching exercises, such as those already discussed earlier in the chapter, which will help to reduce muscle stiffness and soreness. Remember that the body will be warm and the joints and muscles generally more pliable, so stretches can be held for 15 to 20 seconds. The cool-down also provides an opportunity for mental conclusion in the form of dialogue. Discussions should include aspects of the gymnastics lesson and offer opportunities for pupils to recap learnt skills and to invite ideas for the next lesson. Map out the progressions for the next lesson and invite questions that will give you the opportunity to assess your pupils' understanding and gauge their competence before moving on to the next progression.

Dos and Don'ts for the Cool-Down

 ✅ **Do** encourage a slow-paced activity.

 ⊘ **Don't** allow a vigorous activity that will raise the pulse.

- ✓ **Do** encourage static stretching exercises (key stage 2) and whole-body stretches (key stage 1).
- ⊘ **Don't** allow bouncing stretches or vigorous mobility exercises.
- ✓ **Do** discuss how pupils feel physically (and plan adaptations).
- ⊘ **Don't** be dismissive of any comments about physical feelings (such as tired, out of breath, hot, unchallenged).
- ✓ **Do** discuss how pupils feel emotionally (such as happy, thrilled, upset, unsure).
- ⊘ **Don't** be dismissive of any emotional comments.
- ✓ **Do** keep abreast of safety guidelines on exercises.
- ⊘ **Don't** assume current research into safe exercises is conclusive.
- ✓ **Do** encourage good body posture throughout.
- ⊘ **Don't** allow sloppiness in body posture.
- ✓ **Do** include activities that are relevant to the lesson.
- ⊘ **Don't** include activities that are not relevant to the lesson.
- ✓ **Do** focus on mobilisation and stretching of body parts that are relevant to the activity of the lesson (for example, for jump and land activity, stretch the large muscles in legs).
- ⊘ **Don't** focus on mobilisation and stretching of body parts that are not relevant to the activity (for example, mobilising the wrists for a jump and land activity).

Basic Gymnastics Shapes

CHAPTER 6

Basic gymnastics shapes represent the first part of the gymnastics formula:

shape + action = gymnastics skill

The learning and implementation of the five basic gymnastics shapes underpin the development of gymnastics skills throughout this scheme of work and fulfils the primary National Curriculum guidelines, forming a solid foundation from which to assess attainment and improvement. (Refer to chapter 4, Attainment and Assessment.) Knowledge and versatile use of the shapes are attainable to most children; pupils who demonstrate these skills achieve the key strand of acquiring and developing. When pupils are able to add an action, they attain the key strand of selecting and applying. When pupils are able to describe what they observe in their own and others' performances, they attain the key strand of evaluating and improving. If pupils are given the opportunity to discuss and explore how physical activity affects the body and relates to healthy lifestyles, they achieve the key strand of knowledge and understanding of fitness and health.

STRETCH SHAPE

Properties of a Stretch Shape

The stretch shape is long, narrow and tight. It is sometimes referred to as a straight shape; its name reminds pupils to make their bodies as long as possible. The properties of a stretch shape should be evident throughout all attempts:

- The body is narrow and straight from the knees to the shoulders.
- The angle at the hips must remain open (180 degrees).

Teaching Points

Share the following teaching points with your pupils to aid learning and ensure that they achieve these key elements when practising the stretch shape (see figure 6.1):

- Stretch your body and make it as long and narrow as you can.
- Keep legs and feet together.
- Point your toes.

Early Attempts

Pupils' early attempts at the stretch shape often result in the following:

- Bent arms
- Arms not extended above head
- Hands crossing over
- Bent or untidy legs and knees
- Feet and toes not together or pointed
- Lack of tension and extension in the body line
- Angle at the hips not fully extended to 180 degrees

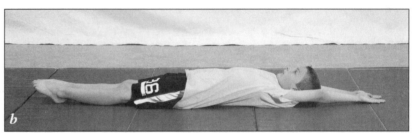

Figure 6.1 *(a)* Stretch shape on feet; *(b)* stretch shape on back; *(c)* stretch shape on front; *(d)* stretch shape on side; *(e)* stretch shape on knees.

 In the Pictorial Resources folder, refer to the Stretch Shape file in the Basic Shapes folder.

Scheme of Work

 The stretch shape appears in most units of work on the DVD.

Gymnastics-Specific Skills

When pupils master the stretch shape, further instruction and guidance will allow them to attempt the following gymnastics skills:

- Stretch roll: Refer to chapter 8, Rolling Techniques. For photos in the Pictorial Resources folder, refer to the Stretch Roll file in the Rolling Techniques folder on the DVD. For videos, in the Dartfish Mediabooks folder, refer to the stretch roll in the Rolling Techniques mediabook.
- Handstand progressions: Refer to chapter 9, Inversions. For photos in the Pictorial Resources folder, refer to the Handstand Progressions file in the Inversions folder. For videos, refer to the Inversions mediabook in the Dartfish Mediabooks folder.
- Stretch jump and land, 180-degree turn jump and land, 360-degree turn jump and land: Refer to the section titled Jumping and Landing in chapter 1, Developing Fundamental Movement Skills Through Gymnastics. For photos in the Pictorial Resources folder, refer to the Spot Landing file in the Flight and Travel folder.

TUCK SHAPE

Properties of a Tuck Shape

The tuck shape is egg-like in appearance. The properties of a tuck shape should be evident throughout all attempts:

- The body is small, rounded and compact.
- The angles at the knees and hips are tight, resulting in the knees being close to the chest and the feet near the buttocks.
- Hands are on shins (where possible).

Teaching Points

Share the following teaching points with your pupils to aid learning and ensure that they achieve these key elements when practising the tuck shape (see figure 6.2):

- Make your body as small as you can.
- Keep legs bent and feet together.
- Bend your arms into your sides.
- Point your toes.
- Put your hands at the top of the shins, just below your knees.

Figure 6.2 *(a)* Tuck shape on buttocks; *(b)* tuck shape on back; *(c)* tuck shape on side; *(d)* tuck shape on knees; *(e)* tuck shape on feet.

Early Attempts

Pupils' early attempts at the tuck shape often result in the following:

- Body not tightly compact
- Knees apart
- Hands not holding tops of shins, but more likely are crossed or hugging the knees
- Elbows stuck out like wings
- Feet crossed
- Ankles and toes not together or pointed

 In the Pictorial Resources folder, refer to the Tuck Shape file in the Basic Shapes folder.

Scheme of Work

 The tuck shape appears in most units of work on the DVD.

Gymnastics-Specific Skills

When pupils master the tuck shape, further instruction and guidance will allow them to attempt the following gymnastics skills:

- Tuck roll: Refer to chapter 8, Rolling Techniques. In the Pictorial Resources folder, refer to the Tuck Roll file in the Rolling Techniques folder. In the Dartfish Mediabooks folder, refer to the tuck roll in the Rolling Techniques mediabook.
- Half roll: Refer to chapter 8, Rolling Techniques. In the Pictorial Resources folder, refer to the Half Roll file in the Rolling Techniques folder. In the Dartfish Mediabooks folder, refer to the half roll in the Rolling Techniques mediabook.
- Bunny jump: Refer to chapter 9, Inversions. In the Pictorial Resources folder, refer to the Handstand Progressions file in the Inversions folder. In the Dartfish Mediabooks folder, refer to the tucked bunny jump clip in the Inversions mediabook.
- Sideways bunny jump: Refer to chapter 9, Inversions. In the Pictorial Resources folder, refer to the Cartwheel Progressions file in the Inversions folder. In the Dartfish Mediabooks folder, refer to the sideways bunny jump clips in the Inversions mediabook.
- Tuck, jump and land: Refer to chapter 1, Developing Fundamental Movement Skills Through Gymnastics, in the section titled Jumping and Landing. In the Pictorial Resources folder, refer to the Spot Landing file in the Flight and Travel folder.
- Tucked vaulted mount position (platform): Refer to chapter 1, Developing Fundamental Movement Skills Through Gymnastics, in the sections titled Running and Jumping and Landing. In the Pictorial Resources folder, refer to the Spot Landing file in the Flight and Travel folder.

STAR SHAPE

Properties of a Star Shape

Younger pupils like to imagine they resemble the stars in the sky. The properties of a star shape should be evident throughout all attempts:

- The body is flat and wide.
- The angle at the hips must remain open (180 degrees).

 Teaching Points

Share the following teaching points with your pupils to aid learning and ensure that they achieve these key elements when practising the star shape (see figure 6.3).

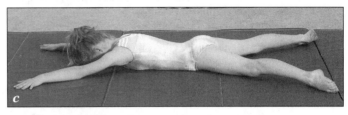

Figure 6.3 *(a)* Star shape on feet; *(b)* star shape on back; *(c)* star shape on front; *(d)* star shape on one hand and one foot.

- Stretch your body and make it as wide and flat as you can.
- Keep legs wide apart.
- Stay flat.
- Point your toes.
- Keep arms straight and wide.

Early Attempts

Pupils' early attempts at the star shape often result in the following:

- Lack of extension in the arms and legs
- Toes not pointed
- Lack of tension and extension in the body line
- Angle at the hips not fully extended to 180 degrees
- Lack of overall width to the shape

 In the Pictorial Resources folder, refer to the Star Shape file in the Basic Shapes folder.

Scheme of Work

 The star shape appears in most units of work on the DVD.

Gymnastics-Specific Skills

When pupils master the star shape, further instruction and guidance will allow them to attempt the following gymnastics skills:

- Cartwheels: Refer to chapter 9, Inversions. In the Pictorial Resources folder, refer to the Cartwheel Progressions file in the Inversions folder. In the Dartfish Mediabooks folder, refer to the sideways bunny jump, bent-leg cartwheel, cartwheel in a rope, and cartwheel clips in the Inversions mediabook.
- Star jump and land: Refer to chapter 1, Developing Fundamental Movement Skills Through Gymnastics, in the section titled Jumping and Landing. In the Pictorial Resources folder, refer to the Spot Landing file in the Flight and Travel folder.

STRADDLE SHAPE

Properties of a Straddle Shape

The straddle shape is an extension of the flat and wide star shape but with an angle (90 degrees or less) at the hips. Younger pupils better associate with the idea of a corner at the hips if they have not yet reached an age where they have learnt about angles. The properties of a straddle shape should be evident throughout all attempts:

- The body is wide.
- The angle at the hips is 90 degrees or less.

Teaching Points

Share the following teaching points with your pupils to aid learning and ensure that they achieve these key elements when practising the straddle shape (see figure 6.4):

- Make sure that there is a right angle (or corner) at your hips.
- Keep legs wide apart.
- Keep legs straight and pointed.
- Point your toes.
- Keep a flat, straight back.
- Keep arms straight and stretched outwards.

Figure 6.4 *(a)* Straddle shape on buttocks; *(b)* straddle shape on back; *(c)* straddle shape on feet.

Early Attempts

Pupils' early attempts at the straddle shape often result in the following:

- Arms not held at horizontal
- Legs not wide enough or sometimes too wide
- Bent and untidy legs and knees
- Legs rolling in at hips
- Feet and toes not pointed
- Rounded back
- Angle at the hips not at 90 degrees or less

 In the Pictorial Resources folder, refer to the Straddle Shape file in the Basic Shapes folder.

Scheme of Work

 The straddle shape appears in most units of work on the DVD.

Gymnastics-Specific Skills

When pupils master the straddle shape, further instruction and guidance will allow them to attempt the following gymnastics skills:

- Straddle roll: Refer to chapter 8, Rolling Techniques. In the Pictorial Resources folder, refer to the Straddle Roll file in the Rolling Techniques folder. In the Dartfish Mediabooks folder, refer to the straddle roll in the Rolling Techniques mediabook.
- Straddle vaulted mount position (platform): Refer to chapter 1, Developing Fundamental Movement Skills Through Gymnastics, in the sections titled Running and Jumping and Landing. In the Pictorial Resources folder, refer to the Spot Landing file in the Flight and Travel folder.

PIKE SHAPE

Properties of a Pike Shape

The pike shape is an extension of the long and narrow stretch shape but with an angle at the hips. The properties of a pike shape should be evident throughout all attempts:

- The body is narrow.
- The angle at the hips is 90 degrees or less.

 Teaching Points

Share the following teaching points with your pupils to aid learning and ensure that they achieve these key elements when practising the pike shape (see figure 6.5):

- Keep arms extended next to the ears
- Try to keep your back flat.
- Keep legs and feet together and straight.
- Point your toes.
- Keep the angle at the hips 90 degrees or less.

Early Attempts

Pupils' early attempts at the pike shape often result in the following:

- Arms not extended next to the ears, but bent and in front of head
- Hands crossing over

Figure 6.5 *(a)* Pike shape on buttocks; *(b)* pike shape on back; *(c)* pike shape on side; *(d)* pike shape on feet; *(e)* pike shape on hands and feet.

- Bent and untidy legs and knees
- Feet and toes not pointed
- Rounded back
- Angle at the hips not at 90 degrees or less

 In the Pictorial Resources folder, refer to the Pike Shape file in the Basic Shapes folder.

Scheme of Work

 The pike shape appears in most units of work on the DVD.

Gymnastics-Specific Skills

There are no gymnastics-specific skills suitable for instruction in primary schools, but pupils may employ the pike shape and add the following actions to the gymnastics lesson:

- Inversion: Refer to the beginning of chapter 9, where a pike shape is used as an example of an inversion skill.
- Balance: Refer to chapter 1, Developing Fundamental Movement Skills Through Gymnastics, in the section titled Balancing. In the Pictorial Resources folder, refer to the Top Postural Shapes file in the Partner Work folder. In the Balance Combinations folder, refer to Basic Shapes for Group Balances, Shape Ideas for Wall Bars and Symmetrical and Asymmetrical Shapes files.
- Travelling: In the Dartfish Mediabooks folder, refer to the implementing basic gymnastics clip in the Rolling Techniques mediabook.
- Jump and land: Refer to chapter 1, Developing Fundamental Movement Skills Through Gymnastics, in the section titled Jumping and Landing. In the Pictorial Resources folder, refer to the Spot Landing file in the Flight and Travel folder.

Note that the stretch, tuck, star (not in partner work) and straddle shapes are also applied in similar ways to the pike shape throughout the scheme of work. In addition, stretching exercises in the straddle and pike shapes are frequently used during the warm-up and cool-down sections of the lesson progressions in the units of work on the DVD.

 Refer to chapter 5, Preparation For and Recovery From Physical Activity. In the Pictorial Resources folder, refer to the Static Stretches file.

CHAPTER

Postural Shapes

7

Postural shapes help to develop core stability by encouraging the muscles of the abdomen and the back to contract and hold the body in a tight, strong shape. The benefits of employing core stability exercises should not be underestimated; these exercises are key to improving body posture, balance skills and agility activities.

BOX SHAPE

Properties of a Box Shape

The box shape is a strong square formed by the body when on the hands and knees (see figure 7.1).

- The back is strong and flat.
- Right angles, or angles of 90 degrees, should be formed at the hips and shoulders.

 **Teaching Points**

Share the following teaching points with your pupils to aid learning and ensure that they achieve these key elements when practising the box shape:

Figure 7.1 Box shape with right angles formed at the hips and shoulders.

- Make the muscles of your abdomen and back very strong
- Arms should be straight with the shoulders directly above the wrists.
- Knees should be positioned directly below the hips.

Early Attempts

Pupils' early attempts at the box often result in a saggy shape, which will prove unstable.

Scheme of Work

 The box is used in the following sections on the DVD:

- Themed Games: Washing the Clothes
- Unit 5: Balances on Large and Small Body Parts Alongside Skipping (year 1 and year 2)
- Unit 10: Partner Up and Roll
- Unit 12: Building Boxes and Bridges
- In the Pictorial Resources folder, refer to the Washing the Clothes files in the Themed Games folder.
- In the Pictorial Resources folder, refer to the Box Shape and Front and Back Supports file in the Postural Shapes folder.
- In the Pictorial Resources folder, refer to the Top Postural Shapes and Box Base Balances files in the Partner Work folder.

FRONT SUPPORT

Properties of a Front Support

The front support is an extension of the box shape and builds on the properties of the stretch shape: long, narrow and tight (see figure 7.2).

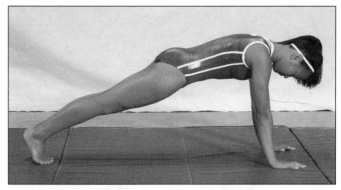

- Stretch shape is on hands and feet, with front towards floor.
- There should be a 90-degree angle at the shoulders.

 Teaching Points

Share the following teaching points with your pupils to aid learning and ensure that they achieve these key elements when practising the front support:

Figure 7.2 Front support with 90-degree angle at the shoulders.

- Make the muscles of your abdomen and back very strong.
- Arms should be straight with the shoulders directly above the wrists.

Early Attempts

Pupils' early attempts at the front support often result in a mountain shape or a banana shape.

Scheme of Work

 The front support is used in the following sections on the DVD:

- Themed Games: Washing the Clothes
- Unit 5: Balances on Large and Small Body Parts Alongside Skipping (year 1 and year 2)
- Unit 10: Partner Up and Roll
- In the Pictorial Resources folder, refer to the Washing the Clothes files in the Themed Games folder.
- In the Pictorial Resources folder, refer to the Box Shape and Front and Back Supports file in the Postural Shapes folder.
- In the Pictorial Resources folder, refer to the Top Postural Shapes file in the Partner Work folder.

BACK SUPPORT

Properties of a Back Support

The back support builds on the properties of the stretch shape: long, narrow and tight (see figure 7.3).

- Stretch shape is on hands and feet, with front towards the ceiling.
- There should be a 90-degree angle at the shoulders.

Figure 7.3 Back support with 90-degree angle at the shoulders.

Teaching Points

Share the following teaching points with your pupils to aid learning and ensure that they achieve these key elements when practising the back support:

- Make the muscles of your abdomen and back very strong.
- The fingers should point towards the feet.

Early Attempts

Pupils' early attempts at the back support often result in a saggy abdomen (the abdomen is not pushed upwards in a straight line).

Scheme of Work

 The back support is used in the following sections on the DVD:

- Themed Games: Washing the Clothes
- Unit 5: Balances on Large and Small Body Parts Alongside Skipping (year 1 and year 2)
- Unit 10: Partner Up and Roll (back support can be used as an alternative to the front support)
- In the Pictorial Resources folder, refer to the Washing the Clothes files in the Themed Games folder.
- In the Pictorial Resources folder, refer to the Box Shape and Front and Back Supports file in the Postural Shapes folder.
- In the Pictorial Resources folder, refer to the Top Postural Shapes file in the Partner Work folder.

ARCH SHAPE

Properties of an Arch

The arch shape is an extension of the basic stretch shape. Use of the arch will increase core stability, thus improving all balance and agility movements (see figure 7.4).

- There is a curved shape on front.
- Hands rest on buttocks before progressing to extending the arms in front of the body.

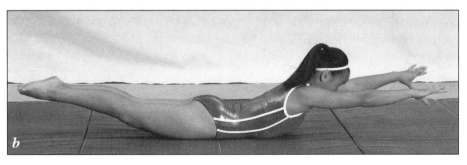

Figure 7.4   Arch shape: (*a*) Hands rest on buttocks. (*b*) Extend arms in front of body.

Teaching Points

Share the following teaching points with your pupils to aid learning and ensure that they achieve these key elements when practising the arch shape:

- Lift your head and shoulders off the floor.
- Lift your legs and arms off the floor, keeping them straight.

Early Attempts

Pupils' early attempts at the arch often result in bent, separated legs.

Scheme of Work

 The arch is used in the following unit of work on the DVD:

- Unit 5: Balances on Large and Small Body Parts Alongside Skipping (year 1 and year 2)
- The arch could also be used as an activity in the cool-down.
- In the Pictorial Resources folder, refer to the Washing the Clothes files in the Themed Games folder.
- In the Pictorial Resources folder, refer to the Arch and Dish Shapes file in the Postural Shapes folder.

DISH SHAPE

Properties of a Dish

The dish shape is an extension of the basic stretch shape: a curved stretch shape on buttocks with hands above thighs. Use of the dish will increase core stability, thus improving all balance and agility movements (see figure 7.5). This shape can be very difficult for pupils to perform correctly; therefore use of the progressions is advised.

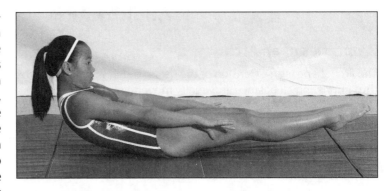

Figure 7.5 The dish shape is a curved stretch shape on buttocks.

 Teaching Points

Strong abdominal muscles are required for performing the dish shape safely and effectively. Share the following teaching points with your pupils to aid learning and ensure that they achieve these key elements when practising the dish shape:

- Hold a tuck shape on buttocks (see figure 7.6a).
- Progress to extending one leg at a time (left leg and then right leg; see figure 7.6b-c).
- Finally extend both legs. Keep looking for your feet and place your hands above your thighs (see figure 7.6d).

Early Attempts

Pupils' early attempts at the dish often result in an arch in the lower back when the legs are extended. If that happens, return to the early progressive steps.

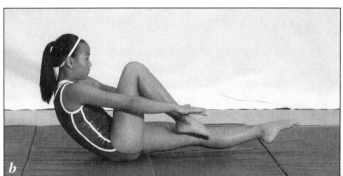

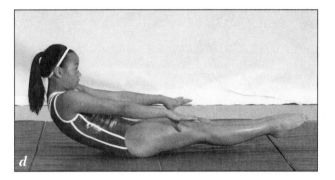

Figure 7.6 Dish shape progression: *(a)* Tuck shape on buttocks; *(b-c)* tuck shape extending one leg; *(d)* final dish shape.

Scheme of Work

The dish shape is used in the following unit of work on the DVD:

- Unit 5: Balances on Large and Small Body Parts Alongside Skipping (year 1 and year 2)
- The dish could also be used as an activity in the cool-down.

- In the Pictorial Resources folder, refer to the Washing the Clothes files in the Themed Games folder.
- In the Pictorial Resources folder, refer to the Arch and Dish Shapes file in the Postural Shapes folder.

Rolling Techniques

As discussed in chapter 1, rolling is one of the first movement patterns a young child performs. In this chapter we develop this movement pattern into gymnastics-specific skills. When developing categories of gymnastics movement, rolling is both a travelling activity and an activity of rotation, and rolling techniques are featured in most of the units of work on the DVD. Information regarding rotation is in chapter 1 of the book. On the DVD in the Pictorial Resources folder, refer to the Rotation file and the Rotation Around an Axis file in the Basic Biomechanics folder for more information.

This resource uses the standard vocabulary for the basic gymnastics shapes. Therefore do not be drawn into referring to certain rolling techniques by their more commonly known nicknames. For example, you may know the stretch roll as a log roll, the tuck roll as an egg roll and the straddle roll as a teddy bear roll. But adopting these names would be a distraction to your gymnastics teaching and a contradiction to the standards of the gymnastics formula. All the rolling techniques in this resource follow the gymnastics formula by employing a basic shape and adding the action of rolling to produce a gymnastics skill. Note that all rolling techniques require the use of mats to ensure pupils' safety. When employing rolling techniques in short compositions, you will advance pupils' understanding of use of space because all the rolls travel. You will also promote the pupils' ability to operate on various levels because the pupils will have to perform the rolls close to the floor.

STRETCH ROLL

Properties of a Stretch Roll

The stretch roll is in a stretch shape and involves the action of rolling in performing a gymnastics-specific skill.

- The body is long and narrow.
- The body rotates a full 360 degrees around the vertical axis.

 Teaching Points

Encourage pupils to maintain a tight and narrow stretch shape to ensure fluid momentum throughout the rolling action. Pupils may choose to start the stretch roll on a different part of the body, such as the front.

- Start position is stretch shape on back (see figure 8.1a).
- Roll into a stretch shape on side (see figure 8.1b).
- Roll into a stretch shape on front (see figure 8.1c).
- Roll into a stretch shape on other side (see figure 8.1d).
- Roll into a finish position of stretch shape on back (see figure 8.1e).

Early Attempts

Pupils' early attempts at the stretch roll often result in the following:

- Arms and legs not in unison while the body rotates
- Arms and legs not extended

Direction of rotation

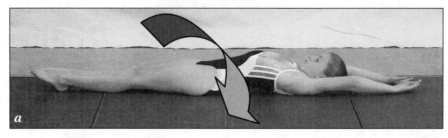

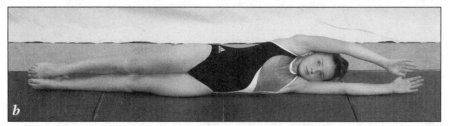

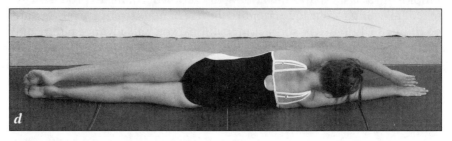

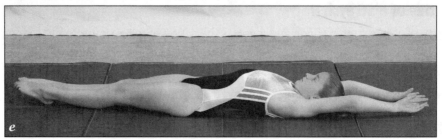

Figure 8.1 Stretch roll: *(a)* start position; *(b)* beginning to roll; *(c)* continuing to roll; *(d)* completing the roll; *(e)* finish position.

- Arms and legs crossing over
- Lack of body tension and coordination
- Lack of fluid momentum causing a bumpy roll

To extend the activities of the stretch roll, you can ask your pupils to implement other basic shapes into the stretch roll. Remember to instruct pupils to roll in the stretch shape, but encourage starting and finishing with the use of different basic gymnastics shapes.

- In the Dartfish Mediabooks folder, refer to the implementing basic gymnastics clip in the Rolling Techniques mediabook.

- In the Pictorial Resources folder, refer to the Stretch Roll file in the Rolling Techniques folder.
- In the Dartfish Mediabooks folder, refer to the stretch roll in the Rolling Techniques mediabook.

Scheme of Work

 Rolling techniques and the stretch roll appear in most units of work on the DVD.

TUCK ROLL

Properties of a Tuck Roll

The tuck roll is in a tuck shape and involves the action of rolling in performing a gymnastics-specific skill.

- The body is compact and rotates 360 degrees around the vertical axis.
- Starting and finishing positions are on the knees.

Teaching Points

Encourage pupils to maintain a tight tuck shape to ensure fluid momentum throughout the rolling action.

- Start position is a high kneeling pose (see figure 8.2a).
- Move into a tuck shape on knees (see figure 8.2b).
- Roll into a tuck shape on side (see figure 8.2c).
- Roll into a tuck shape on back (see figure 8.2d).
- Roll into a tuck shape on other side (see figure 8.2e).
- Roll into a tuck shape on knees (see figure 8.2f).
- Move to finish position of a high kneeling pose (see figure 8.2g).

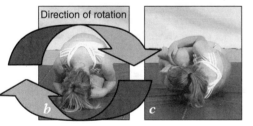

Figure 8.2 Tuck roll: *(a)* start position; *(b)* adopt shape for roll; *(c)* beginning to roll; *(d)* continuing to roll; *(e)* completing the roll; *(f)* maintain shape from roll; *(g)* finish position.

Early Attempts

Pupils' early attempts at the tuck roll often result in the following:

- Not rolling in a straight line
- Lack of maintenance of the tuck shape

To extend the activities of the tuck roll, you can ask pupils to implement other basic shapes into the roll. Remember to instruct pupils to roll in the tuck shape but encourage punctuating the middle of the roll by using a different shape.

- In the Dartfish Mediabooks folder, refer to the implementing shapes tuck roll clip in the Rolling Techniques mediabook.
- In the Pictorial Resources folder, refer to the Tuck Roll file in the Rolling Techniques folder.
- In the Dartfish Mediabooks folder, refer to the tuck roll in the Rolling Techniques mediabook.

Scheme of Work

Rolling techniques and the tuck roll appear in most units of work on the DVD.

SIDE ROLL

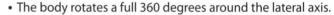

Properties of a Side Roll

The side roll starts and finishes in a star shape but changes to a straddle shape during the action of rolling in performing a gymnastics-specific skill.

- The body is wide throughout.
- The body rotates a full 360 degrees around the lateral axis.

Teaching Points

Encourage pupils to maintain a solid straddle shape to ensure fluid momentum throughout the rolling action.

- Start position is a high kneeling pose in a star shape (see figure 8.3a).
- Move the arm on the bent-leg side of the body across the body and roll onto the upper back and shoulder and continue to roll in a straddle shape on back (see figure 8.3b).
- Roll to finish position in a high kneeling pose with one leg bent and the other leg in a star shape (see figure 8.3c).

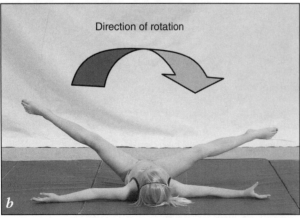

Figure 8.3 Side roll: (a) start position; (b) rolling; (c) finish position.

Early Attempts

Pupils' early attempts at the side roll often result in the following:

- Not rolling in a straight line
- Lack of maintenance of the straddle shape on back
- Untidy legs
- Lack of awareness of arm position throughout

- In the Pictorial Resources folder, refer to the Side Roll file in the Rolling Techniques folder.

- In the Dartfish Mediabooks folder, refer to the side roll in the Rolling Techniques mediabook.

Scheme of Work

The side roll appears in unit 16 (Rock, Roll and Invert) in the Lateral Axis section.

HALF ROLL

Properties of a Half Roll

The half roll is a tuck shape that involves the action of rolling in performing a gymnastics-specific skill. The body starts and finishes in a stretch shape on feet and adopts the compact tuck shape when rotating around the horizontal axis in a backwards-and-forwards motion.
   Progressive steps include

- the body rocks repetitively backwards and forwards in the tuck shape (buttocks to shoulders to buttocks) before attempting to start from an upright position, and
- pupils can join with a partner and help them by holding hands on the rise to stand.

☆ Teaching Points

Encourage your pupils to maintain a tuck shape to ensure fluid momentum throughout the rolling action. To assist pupils, instruct them to place the chin on the chest to maintain the curved shape of the back. As noted in the early attempts, younger pupils may find it easier to place their hands on their shins to maintain the tuck shape. This is an acceptable and safe practice until a pupil becomes strong enough to maintain the shape without the assistance of holding on to the knees.

- Start position is the stretch shape on feet. Use of the arms is optional, but it is easier if the arms are held forwards at horizontal (see figure 8.4a).
- Sit into a tuck shape on buttocks (see figure 8.4b).
- Roll into a tuck shape on back (see figure 8.4c).
- Continue rolling backwards into a tuck shape on shoulders (see figure 8.4d).
- Roll forwards into a tuck shape on buttocks (see figure 8.4e).
- Continue rolling forwards into a tuck shape on feet (see figure 8.4f).
- Rise to stand in finish position of stretch shape on feet (see figure 8.4g).

Early Attempts

Pupils' early attempts at the half roll often result in the following:

- Inability to sit down confidently without using hands
- Not rolling in a straight line or rolling onto side of body
- Lack of maintenance of the tuck shape (hands may be required to maintain the shape)
- Lack of fluid momentum causing a bumpy roll
- Inability to stand up without using hands or without crossing feet

   To extend the activities of the half roll, you can ask pupils to finish the half roll in the start position of a different roll, such as the tuck roll or straddle roll. Remember to instruct pupils to complete the half roll before adopting a different finish position.

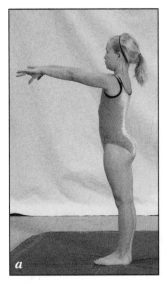
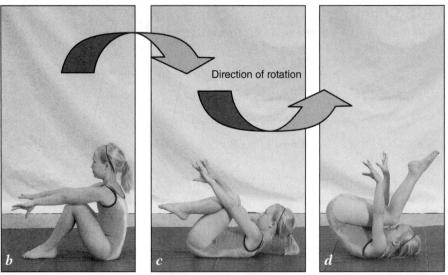

Direction of rotation

Figure 8.4 Half roll: *(a)* start position; *(b)* descending to adopt shape for roll; *(c)* rolling backwards; *(d)* continuing to roll backwards; *(e)* rolling forwards; *(f)* completing the roll; *(g)* finish position.

• In the Dartfish Mediabooks folder, refer to the half roll, tuck roll and half roll, and straddle roll in the Rolling Techniques mediabook.

• In the Pictorial Resources folder, refer to the Half Roll file in the Rolling Techniques folder.

• In the Dartfish Mediabooks folder, refer to the half roll in the Rolling Techniques mediabook.

Scheme of Work

Rolling techniques and the half roll appear in most units of work on the DVD.

STRADDLE ROLL

Properties of a Straddle Roll

The straddle roll is in a straddle shape that involves the action of rolling in performing a gymnastics-specific skill. The body is wide and angled 90 degrees at the hips and rotates 180 degrees around the vertical axis.

Progressive steps include the body rocking repetitively backwards and forwards in the straddle shape (buttocks to shoulders to buttocks) before attempting to change direction.

⭐ Teaching Points

Encourage pupils to maintain a solid straddle shape to ensure fluid momentum throughout the rolling action.

- Start position is straddle shape on buttocks (see figure 8.5*a*). Before you begin to roll, place hands behind knees to maintain straddle shape throughout skill.
  - Roll into a straddle shape on side (see figure 8.5*b*).
  - Roll into a straddle shape on back (see figure 8.5*c*).
  - Roll into a straddle shape on the other side (see figure 8.5*d*).
  - Finish position is a straddle shape on buttocks, facing the opposite direction to that of the start position (see figure 8.5*e*).

Direction of rotation

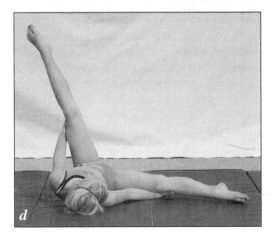

Figure 8.5 Straddle roll: *(a)* start position; *(b)* beginning to roll; *(c)* continuing to roll; *(d)* completing the roll; *(e)* finish position.

Early Attempts

Pupils' early attempts at the straddle roll often result in the following:

- Not rolling and rotating (unable to change direction)
- Lack of maintenance of the straddle shape (legs bending and closing)
- Lack of awareness to roll only on broad back area of body

To extend the activities of the straddle roll, you can ask your pupils to choose a partner to perform a straddle roll with. Pupils should sit back to back with a partner and then on cue straddle roll at the same time. Remember to instruct the pupils to go in the same direction (for example, both pupils should roll to their right to prevent them becoming tangled).

- In the Pictorial Resources folder, refer to the Straddle Roll file in the Rolling Techniques folder.
- In the Dartfish Mediabooks folder, refer to the straddle roll in the Rolling Techniques mediabook.

Scheme of Work

Rolling techniques and the straddle roll appear in most units of work on the DVD.

FORWARD ROLL

Properties of a Forward Roll

The forward roll involves the action of rolling through many basic shapes to achieve a gymnastics-specific skill. The body is long and narrow at the start, then forms a small rounded shape where the legs extend to create rotation and then bend again to stand up and complete the roll. Rotation occurs around the horizontal axis.

The forward roll is a skill that teachers often consider high risk. A forward roll is a safe gymnastics skill, but the National Curriculum does not stipulate its inclusion in the curriculum; therefore you should instruct the forward roll only if you are confident in doing so. Many pupils voluntarily include forward rolls in their sequences; therefore an understanding of the skill is advised.

Here are some facts to keep in mind regarding the forward roll:

- Some children are genuinely frightened to perform a forward roll.
- To rotate and roll, the body needs to fall out of balance, which can be scary.
- Some children do not like to go upside down.

Teaching Points

Because of the complexities of forward rolling with complete technical accuracy, the forward roll is divided into two progressions: learning and performing. It is unlikely that pupils will achieve a technically accurate forward roll within the confines of the time allowed and the supervision available to most teachers in a primary physical edcation environment. Safety is a high priority when instructing a forward roll, and the following learning process is the recognised safe method that I have used with success when instructing a class for the first time. The learning of the forward roll progressions is an easy step for you to instruct and for pupils to safely achieve the initial rotation process.

Learning the Forward Roll

Instruct your pupils carefully on the safety guidelines so that they are able to make informed choices when learning the forward roll. Explain the importance of tucking the head in and pressing the hands into the floor to ensure a safe approach.

- Start position is like that of a star shape: legs apart with arms stretched upwards (see figure 8.6a).
- Bend at the hips and place the hands on the floor in line with and close to the feet (see figure 8.6b).
- Press on the hands, tuck the chin into the chest and look through the hole to initiate the rolling action (see figure 8.6c).
- Roll onto the upper back and continue to roll forwards and return to standing by bending the legs and reaching the arms forward. Finish position is a stretch shape on feet.
- Important safety guidelines and teaching points include ensuring that the chin is tucked into the chest and the hands are pressed into the floor to help support the roll.
- If a pupil is genuinely afraid to forward roll, he will usually place the hands a long way in front of the feet at the start, thus providing a barrier to rotation (see figure 8.6d).

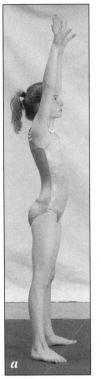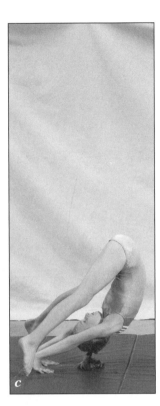

Figure 8.6 Learning the forward roll: *(a)* start position; *(b)* adopting the shape to allow rotation to take place; *(c)* beginning to roll; *(d)* pupil has placed their hands a long way in front of their feet suggesting they are not confident to attempt the roll forwards.

• In the Pictorial Resources folder, refer to the Learning the Forward Roll file in the Rolling Techniques folder.

• In the Dartfish Mediabooks folder, refer to learning the forward roll in the Rolling Techniques mediabook.

Progression to performing the forward roll will occur only when pupils are confident and competent to do this with ease and without anxiety. Remember that some children are genuinely frightened to perform a forward roll. Therefore, if pupils only achieve the skills akin to learning the forward roll, they will have achieved a safe sport-specific skill but one that is just not technically accurate. The correct techniques in performing an accurate forward roll are explained in the following section. To appreciate the technical progression, you should note the difference in body shapes used at the beginning of the roll and the methods used in initiating the rolling action.

Performing the Forward Roll

The forward roll should have fluid momentum and display a level of measured speed initiated by the straightening of the legs at the start of the skill.

• Start position is a stretch shape on feet (see figure 8.7*a*).

• Bend the legs into a tuck shape on feet with the arms extended upwards (see figure 8.7*b*).

• Place the hands on the floor in a tuck shape and place the chin on the chest (see figure 8.7*c*).

• Press on the hands, tuck the chin into the chest and push the legs straight to initiate the rolling action, briefly passing through the pike shape (see figure 8.7*d*).

• Roll forwards onto the shoulders and back beginning to bend the legs (see figure 8.7 *e-f*).

• Roll forwards onto the buttocks in a tuck shape (see figure 8.7*g*).

• Roll forwards onto the feet in a tuck shape to stand up, arms reaching forward (see figure 8.7*h*).

• Finish position is a stretch shape on feet (see figure 8.7*i*).

Direction of rotation

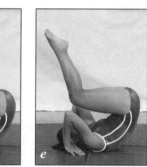

Figure 8.7 Forward roll: *(a)* start position; *(b)* adopt shape to initiate rolling; *(c)* secure safety procedures; *(d-f)* rolling; *(g)* completing the roll; *(h)* rising to stand; *(i)* finish position.

Early Attempts

Pupils' early attempts at the forward roll often result in the following:

- Not rolling in a straight line
- Trying to place the top of the head on the mat instead of tucking the head in by placing the chin on the chest
- Untidy legs throughout the roll
- Using the hands or crossing the legs to help stand up

- In the Pictorial Resources folder, refer to the Forward Roll file in the Rolling Techniques folder.

- In the Dartfish Mediabooks folder, refer to the forward roll in the Rolling Techniques mediabook.

Scheme of Work

This sport-specific skill is not specified in a unit of work, but you may see pupils attempting the forward roll when asked to include rolling techniques in composing their own sequences.

CHAPTER

Inversions 9

I n gymnastics, an inversion skill occurs when the hips are raised above the level of the head. Inversions are divided into different categories of gymnastics skills: static balances (such as the bridge and handstand) and travelling skills (as demonstrated by the cartwheel). An example of a simple inversion is a pike shape on hands and feet, as shown in figure 9.1.

I usually teach the handstand inversion skill before the cartwheel because it promotes body management and advances pupils' orientation experience of being upside down before progressing to the more complicated skill of a cartwheel. Note that all gymnastics-specific inversions require the use of mats to ensure pupils' safety. Pupils will have many opportunities to turn upside down when asked to explore activities from the various units of work on the DVD.

Figure 9.1 Inversion in pike position.

BRIDGE

Properties of a Bridge

This gymnastics-specific skill is a complex move and requires both strength in the shoulders and arms to push the head off the floor and mobility in the shoulders to enable the arms to fully extend over the head. In most gymnastics lessons there will be pupils who attempt to perform the bridge. You should have adequate knowledge to oversee the skill before your pupils attempt the bridge.

Learning the bridge is dependent on a child's physical maturity. The arms have to be long enough to extend over the head comfortably to enable the child lift the head off the mat. Refer to the information in chapter 1 regarding the differences in the body shapes of a child and an adult.

 ### Teaching Points

Share the following teaching points with your pupils to aid learning and ensure that they achieve these key elements when practicing the bridge:

- Start position is stretch shape on back (see figure 9.2*a*).
- Position the hands under the shoulders with fingers pointing towards the feet (see figure 9.2*b*).
- Bend the legs so that the feet are tucked up flat near the buttocks. There may be a small space between the feet (see figure 9.2*b*).
- Push on the feet and hands and drive the hips upwards by straightening the legs (see figure 9.2*c*).
- Push the head off the mat by straightening the arms (see figure 9.2*c*).
- Return to stretch shape on back by tucking the chin into the chest. *Do not* place the top of the head onto the mat when exiting the skill.
- Stretch the arms and legs out to full extension.

Encourage your pupils to curl up into a tuck shape and rock backwards and forwards a few times to stretch the back after each attempt.

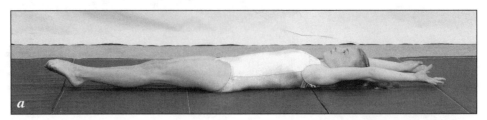

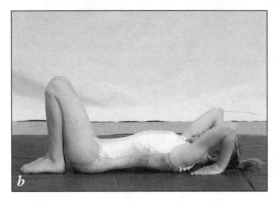

Figure 9.2 Bridge: (*a*) Start in stretch shape on back. (*b*) Place hands near ears and flat feet near buttocks. (*c*) Push on feet and hands and drive hips upwards to make bridge.

Early Attempts

Pupils' early attempts at the bridge often result in the following:

- Head not lifting off the floor
- Arms and legs very wide
- Hands and feet not flat on the floor
- Arms remaining bent even when head is off the floor
- Shoulders not over the wrists when head is off the floor and arms are straight

 In the Pictorial Resources folder, refer to the Bridge file in the Inversions folder.

Scheme of Work

The bridge is featured in unit 12 (Building Boxes and Bridges).

HANDSTAND

Properties of a Handstand

Handstands are technically a balance skill and should be approached in the same manner as all balances with an emphasis on control, focus and tightness. Technically a handstand is a stretch shape on the hands, but this is very hard to achieve. During instruction, all the progressions should ensure maximum safety throughout. Take into consideration that most pupils will not progress past the half handstand.

Here are some facts to keep in mind regarding the handstand:

- Some children do not like to go upside down!
- Some children are genuinely frightened to take weight on their hands.

☆ Teaching Points

A simplified example of a handstand can be achieved by asking pupils to stand with their backs towards a wall or piece of large apparatus (platforms or wall bars), place the hands on the floor and walk the feet up the apparatus raising the hips above the head. Ensure that pupils focus on the space between the hands and keep the arms straight throughout. Mats are required for this activity. (See unit 16: Rock, Roll and Invert in the scheme of work on the DVD.)

Bunny Jump

- The bunny jump is a tuck shape on hands (see figure 9.3c).

- Repeat and rehearse the bunny jump to familiarize pupils with turning upside down and supporting their body weight on their hands and arms.
- The bunny jump should be performed with control and good body management. Ensure that the tuck shape is maintained throughout.
- When pupils achieve competence of this simple inversion, you may ask them to continue to the next progression.

Figure 9.3 Bunny jump progression for the handstand: *(a)* Start position is a tuck shape on feet with the arms extended forwards. *(b)* Place the hands on the mat. *(c)* Make a small and controlled jump to lift the hips in the air. *Do not* allow the feet to lead the way. *(d)* Finish position is a tuck shape on feet with the arms extended forwards.

Entrance and Exit

- Problems occur when pupils put lots of energy into the entrance of a handstand and then fall out uncontrollably on the exit.
- It may be necessary to teach just the entrance and exit of a handstand first, emphasising the need to keep on the *safe side* of the skill. (see figure 9.4).

Safe side

Figure 9.4 Safe entrance and exit progression for the handstand: *(a)* Start position is an upright stance with the arms held upwards and with the preferred leg extended and pointed forwards. *(b)* Lift the preferred leg take a step forwards, making a lunge position. *(c)* Place the hands onto the mat whilst lifting the back leg with control, then push on the floor with the hands to return to an upright stance. *(d)* Finish position is an upright stance with the arms held upwards and with the preferred leg extended and pointed forwards.

- Highlight the dangers of falling into the unsafe side of the skill, which is difficult to manage and caused by a lack of control. Ensure that pupils understand the spatial areas that constitute the *safe side* and *unsafe side* of a handstand and appreciate the dangers of inverting without control.
- When pupils achieve competence in entering and exiting the handstand, you may ask them to continue to the next progression.

Half Handstand

- Extend the entrance and exit skill to allow the pushing leg to lift off the floor slightly (see figure 9.5d).
- As pupils gain confidence, the leg can lift higher (maximum height is horizontal).
- During the inversion phase, focus on the mat between the hands.
- Do not allow pupils to fall onto the *unsafe side*. Place an emphasis on control.
- *Do not* allow pupils to kick and lift the base leg too high off the floor or to change legs in the air, thus returning to the floor with the other leg leading. Emphasise the three key elements of a static balance: control, focus and tight.
- When pupils achieve competence in the half handstand, you may ask them to continue to the next progression.

Figure 9.5 Half-handstand progression for the full handstand: *(a)* Start position is an upright stance with the arms held upwards and with the preferred leg extended and pointed forwards. *(b)* Lift the preferred leg and take a step forwards, making a lunge position. *(c)* Place the hands onto the mat whilst lifting the back leg with control. *(d)* Press on the hands and with control push off the front leg, lifting it slightly off the floor. *(e)* Return the foot to the mat with control. *(f)* Push on the mat to return to an upright stance. *(g)* Finish position is an upright stance with the arms held upwards and with the preferred leg extended and pointed forwards.

Handstand

- As pupils gain confidence, ask them to tap their feet together as soon as they can between the horizontal and vertical planes, ensuring that they remain on the *safe side*.
- During the inversion phase, focus on the mat between the hands.
- As they gain poise, the pupils will gradually progress to rotating the full 180 degrees to perform the handstand, a stretch shape on hands (see figure 9.6*d*).
- Continue to emphasise the three key elements of a static balance: control, focus and tight.

  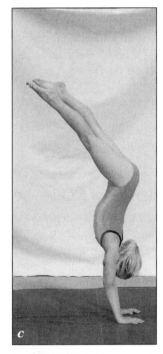 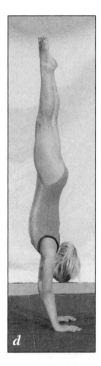

Figure 9.6 Progression for the full handstand: *(a)* Start position is an upright stance with the arms held upwards and with the preferred leg extended and pointed forwards. *(b)* Lift the preferred leg and take a step forwards, making a lunge position. *(c)* Press on the hands and with control lift the back leg; push off the front leg and lift it to join and tap the top leg briefly. *(d)* Gradually with confidence, the body will straighten out with the legs joining in an inverted position to perform a handstand. *(e)* Exit the handstand by lowering the preferred leg onto the mat. *(f)* Finish position is an upright stance with the arms held upwards and with the preferred leg extended and pointed forwards.

Early Attempts

Pupils' early attempts at the handstand often result in the following:

- Entering the handstand without control (no start position)
- Exiting the handstand without control (no finish position)
- Not focusing the eyes on the mat at the space between the hands
- Untidy and bent legs
- Entering and exiting the handstand using different legs

- In the Pictorial Resources folder, refer to the Handstand Progressions file in the Inversions folder.
- In the Dartfish Mediabooks folder, refer to the handstand progressions in the Inversions mediabook.

Scheme of Work

The handstand is featured in unit 16 (Rock, Roll and Invert).

CARTWHEEL

Properties of a Cartwheel

A cartwheel is both an inversion skill and a travelling skill. The cartwheel is traditionally performed in a star shape that starts on the feet, rotates onto the hands and finishes on the feet. Taking into consideration the properties of a star shape (flat and wide), this can be a very difficult shape to control and maintain through 360 degrees of rotation. Therefore most pupils will not achieve technically accurate cartwheels in the time available during most curricular lessons. Cartwheels also require the performer to have a reasonable level of coordination and spatial awareness, leaving some to feel disorientated and confused during early attempts.

Here are some facts to keep in mind regarding the cartwheel:

- Most pupils' preferred leg to lead into a cartwheel will be the same as the hand they write with.
- Some pupils might prefer to lead with the other leg. That is, some pupils are right handed but left legged.
- Right-legged pupils should place the hands onto the right side of the mat, and left-legged pupils should place the hands onto the left side of the mat.
- When pupils lead with one leg (such as the right leg) but place their hands onto the other side of the mat (left side), suggest first attempting to lead with the other leg (left leg) because management of the upper body in a young pupil is usually more dominant than that of the lower limbs. Refer to chapter 1 for the information regarding cephalocaudal development.
- It is easier to control and coordinate a small body shape (tucked bunny jumps, bent-leg cartwheel progressions) rather than a large body shape when learning to coordinate the pattern of hands and feet in a cartwheel.

Teaching Points

A simplified example of a cartwheel can be achieved by asking pupils to transfer the body from one side of a bench to the other by taking weight on the hands in a similar movement to a sideways bunny jump. Mats are not required for this activity.

Sideways Bunny Jump

- The sideways bunny jump enables the pupil to learn to transfer body weight from one place to another using the arms as support (see figure 9.7).
- In these first progressions, encourage pupils to focus on the mat at the space between their hands and to turn their bodies 180 degrees during the movement pattern as they transfer the body from one area of the mat to a different area of the mat. If pupils follow both these instructions, they will not become disorientated or fall out of control.

Figure 9.7 Sideways bunny jump progression for a cartwheel: *(a)* Start position is a tuck shape on feet with the arms held forwards at horizontal to aid balance. *(b)* Place the hands onto one side of the mat. *(c)* Perform a small jump to move the body from one side of the hands to the other side of the hands whilst keeping the arms straight. *(d)* The feet land on the mat on the other side of the hands. *(e)* Finish position is a tuck shape on feet facing the direction the pupil has travelled from, with the arms held forwards at horizontal to aid balance.

- When pupils achieve competence in the sideways bunny jump, you may ask them to continue to the next progression.

Step Into Sideways Bunny Jump

- Introducing a step into the sideways bunny jump enables the pupils to decide which will be their preferred leg (see figure 9.8). If complications arise concerning which leg to use or which side of the mat the hands should be placed, encourage pupils to follow the placing of their hands. You can expect some confusion here, but do not worry!

Figure 9.8 Stepping into sideways bunny jump progression for a cartwheel: *(a)* Start position is an upright stance with the arms held upwards and with the preferred leg extended and pointed forwards. *(b)* Place the hands onto one side of the mat. *(c)* Push from the leg to move the body in a tuck shape from one side of the hands to the other side of the hands whilst keeping the arms straight. *(d)* The feet land together on the mat on the other side of the hands. *(e)* Finish position is a tuck shape on feet facing the direction the pupil has travelled from with the arms held forwards at horizontal to aid balance.

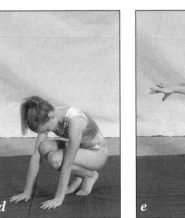

• When pupils achieve competence in stepping into the sideways bunny jump, you may ask them to continue to the next progression.

Bent-Leg Cartwheel

• Encourage pupils to finish in the traditional cartwheel shape of the star. At this stage the legs can remain bent (remember it is easier to control a smaller body area; see figure 9.9).

• Pupils can also practice the bent-leg cartwheel over a bench.

• When pupils achieve competence in the bent-leg cartwheel, you may ask them to continue to the next progression.

Figure 9.9 Bent-leg cartwheel progression for the full cartwheel: *(a)* Start position is an upright stance with the arms held upwards and with the preferred leg extended and pointed forwards. *(b)* Place the hands onto one side of the mat. *(c)* Push from the leg to move the body from one side of the hands to the other side of the hands whilst keeping the arms straight. *(d)* The feet land one at a time on the mat on the other side of the hands. *(e)* Finish position is a star shape on feet facing sideways.

Cartwheel

Once pupils achieve orientation and coordination of the bent-leg cartwheel skill, you can ask them to straighten their legs and to start and finish in the traditional cartwheel star shape (see figure 9.10).

Cartwheels can also be practiced within the confines of an arched rope or conveniently placed beanbags to encourage the correct foot–hand–hand–foot placements (see figure 9.11).

Early Attempts

Pupils' early attempts at the cartwheel often result in the following:

• Entering the cartwheel without control (no start position)
• Exiting the cartwheel without control (no finish position)
• Confusion about which leg to use and which side of the mats to place hands
• Untidy and bent legs
• Landing on the knees or other body parts, which is not a safe alternative to landing on the feet
• Not focusing the eyes on the floor at the space between the hands

Figure 9.10 Cartwheel: *(a)* Start position is a star shape on feet facing sideways. *(b)* The middle phase of the cartwheel shows an inverted star shape. *(c)* Finish position is a star shape on feet facing sideways.

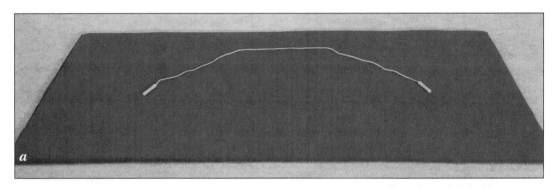

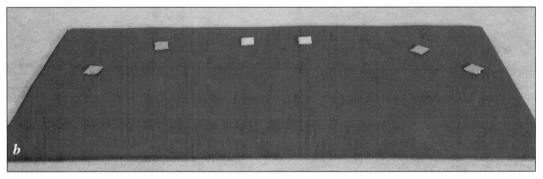

Figure 9.11 *(a)* Arched rope *(b)* or beanbags can help with learning the correct foot–hand–hand–foot placements of a cartwheel.

- In the Pictorial Resources folder, refer to the Cartwheel Progressions file in the Inversions folder.
- In the Dartfish Mediabooks folder, refer to the cartwheel progressions, cartwheel in a rope, and cartwheel in the Inversions mediabook.

Scheme of Work

 The cartwheel is featured in unit 16 (Rock, Roll and Invert).

CHAPTER

Partner Work 10

Working with a partner in gymnastics is fun and allows for team building and cooperative social skills to develop. In key stage 3 of gymnastics, the pupils are usually expected to take part in partner work, so an introduction in key stage 2 at primary school will better prepare them for these later challenges and help to bridge the gap from gymnastics expectations in key stage 2 to gymnastics expectations in key stage 3. Before embarking on partner work in the form of paired balances, both you and your pupils should be familiar with the following vocabulary guidelines and the health and safety instructions.

Base and Top: Who Is Who?

The partner who controls the supporting and partial lifting is referred to as the base. The partner who is being supported and partially lifted is referred to as the top (see figure 10.1). You and your pupils should learn to refer to these positions using the correct vocabulary.

Figure 10.1 Base and top positions in a paired balance.

Partners should be of a similar size, allowing for each partner to swap roles. Therefore, each has the opportunity to be a base and a top. If a situation arises where the pupils are unevenly sized, the smaller pupil should *always* be the top. Always instruct the partners that they are now responsible for each other and should have consideration for the other person at all times. Verbal communication is vital in sharing information. The base usually leads and permits the beginning and the end of the paired balance. In your instructions, you should tell the base that once in position, he or she should not move until the top has completed the balance.

Scheme of Work

 Partner work is featured in three units of work on the DVD. Once learnt, partner balances may be implemented when you ask pupils to compose sequences from other units of work.

- Unit 10: Partner Up and Roll
- Unit 12: Building Boxes and Bridges
- Unit 14: Push, Pull and Skip

TOP POSTURAL SHAPES

Properties of Top Postural Shapes

All the paired balances in this category are built on previously learnt skills from the categories of basic gymnastics shapes and postural shapes.

- Basic gymnastics shapes of stretch, tuck, pike and straddle shapes and the postural shape of the box provide the base position in the paired balances.
- Postural shapes of the front support and back support provide the top position in all the paired balances.

 Teaching Points

The paired balances shown here are not the only skills possible, and you should encourage your pupils to explore more variations.

Entry, Execution and Exit Guidelines

- The base takes up position choosing from one of the basic gymnastics shapes (stretch, tuck, straddle or pike) or the postural shape (box) (see figure 10.2).
- Top stands a measured distance from the base either facing towards or facing away from the base and ensures that the base is stable.
- Top prepares to take up the postural shape of the front support. A back support may be used as an alternative.
- Control, focus, tight: This is the formula for the safe performance of all static balance skills.
- Top places hands on the floor and with control gently places the feet onto the base's back, shoulders or hands to take up the front support position. The ankles of the top should be extended so that they are flat when positioned onto the base.
- Balance is held for 3 seconds.
- Top descends from the balance onto the feet to return to an upright position.

Figure 10.2 Paired balances: *(a)* tuck shape and front support; *(b)* stretch shape and front support; *(c)* pike shape and front support; *(d)* straddle shape and front support.

Early Attempts

Pupils' early attempts at the top postural shape often result in the following:

- Poor execution of basic gymnastics shapes
- Poor execution of the front support postural shape, displaying either a mountain (buttocks up) or a banana (buttocks down) effect
- Base moving thus displaying instability
- Top entering and exiting the balance from the knees instead of from an upright position
- Distance between base and top either too close or too far apart

 In the Pictorial Resources folder, refer to the Top Postural Shapes file in the Partner Work folder.

BOX BASE BALANCES

Properties of Box Base Balances

All the paired balances are built on previously learnt skills from the categories of basic gymnastics shapes and postural shapes. Creative ideas are encouraged as well (see figure 10.3).

The postural shape of the box provides the base position for all the partner balances in this category. The top positions in this category of partner balances are chosen from the following:

- Basic gymnastics shape: Top performs the star shape.
- Postural shape: Top performs the front support.
- Creative idea: Top performs the stag shape.

Figure 10.3 Demonstrating a creative idea: stag shape.

Teaching Points

The box is used as the base position; the top performs the front support, star and stag shapes in the following selection of balances (see figure 10.4). The paired balances shown here are not the only skills possible; you should encourage your pupils to explore more variations.

Entry, Execution and Exit Guidelines

- Base secures box shape with a strong, straight back, flat hands and straight arms. Knees may be slightly parted to increase base surface area and aid stability (see figure 10.5).
- Top stands a measured distance from the base either facing towards or facing away from the base and ensures that the base is stable.
- Control, focus, tight: This is the formula for the safe performance of all balance skills.
- Top carefully takes up position partially supported by the base. The top should ensure at least one limb remains in contact with the floor at all times.
- Balance is held for 3 seconds.
- Top descends from the balance onto the feet to return to an upright position.

Early Attempts

Pupils' early attempts at the box base balances often result in the following:

- Poor execution of basic gymnastics shapes, postural shapes or creative ideas
- Poor execution of the box postural shape

Figure 10.4 Box base balances: *(a)* box and star shape; *(b)* box and front support; *(c)* box and stag; *(d)* box and arched stag.

- Top entering and exiting the balance without displaying the control, focus or tight balance formula
- Top not keeping a limb or multiple limbs in contact with the floor at all times to aid the base in supporting his or her own body weight

 In the Pictorial Resources folder, refer to the Box Base Balances file in the Partner Work folder.

Figure 10.5 Showing correct execution of the box.

COUNTERBALANCE AND COUNTERTENSION

Properties of Counterbalance and Countertension

Counterbalance and countertension skills require the ultimate cooperation and trust where each person in the partnership is directly responsible for supporting their partner's weight to secure the safe maintenance of the counterbalance or countertension paired balance. The partners share equal responsibilities and roles; there is no base or top position. If one person moves unexpectedly, or the centre of mass is not directly over the base, the balance will become unstable and may collapse.

All counterbalance and countertension skills build on the principles of stability and balance. Pupils need to know where their centre of mass is and how it can move according to the shape of the body. For example, the centre of mass can fall outside the perimeter of the body to enable you to remain in balance. Rehearse the basic rules of stability and balance. Have pupils explore locating their centre of mass during different body shapes. Information regarding balance and stability and locating your centre of mass is in chapter 1.

- In the Pictorial Resources folder, refer to the files in the Balance Combinations folder.
- In the Basic Biomechanics folder, refer to the Where Is My Centre of Mass? file and the Stability and Balance file.

Teaching Points

- There are two types of counter-activities: counterbalances and countertensions.
- Counterbalance can be achieved by using the pushing method, which produces a pyramid shape. Pushing balances require the partners to form a wide base that narrows at the top of the balance. Following basic rules of stability and balance, the pushing counterbalances should be easier than the pulling countertensions because of the wide and more stable base position.
- Countertension can be achieved by using the pulling method, which produces a V-shape. Pulling balances require the partners to have a narrow base that gradually extends to a broader top. Following basic rules of stability and balance, the pulling countertensions should be harder than the pushing counterbalances because of the narrow and less stable base position.
- The wrist grip is important for the safe practice of all pulling countertension skills. You should instruct pupils on the proper wrist grip before they attempt any pulling countertension activity (see figure 10.6).

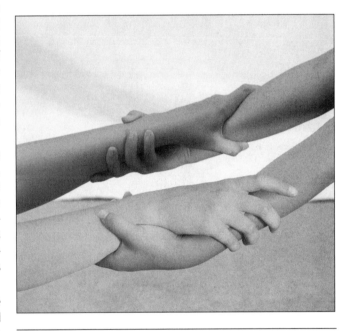

Figure 10.6 For safety, pupils should practice the proper wrist grip technique with a partner before attempting any pulling countertension skills.

Counterbalance

The paired balances shown in this section are not the only skills possible, and you should encourage your pupils to explore other variations. First, experiment with the action of pushing by instructing pupils in the following Back to Back, Push to Stand (Pushing) activity:

- Select a partner of a similar size.
- Sit on the floor back to back with your knees bent (tuck shape on buttocks).
- Link arms with your partner at the elbows.
- Push against each other, and help each other to stand up, forming a pyramid shape.
- Do not move the feet, and keep pushing against each other to maintain balance.
- Reverse the process, and return to the sitting position.

Entry, Execution and Exit Guidelines

- Partners position themselves apart with the body parts that will form the base of the pyramid at a suitable distance apart.

- Control, focus, tight: This is the formula for the safe performance of all balance skills.

- Partners lean inwards and at the connected parts of the body push very slowly with control to form a pyramid shape.

- Balance is held for 3 seconds.

- Partners return from the balance by pushing each other back to an upright position.

Ask pupils to try to counterbalance with their partner by connecting with the following parts of the body. This will alter the appearance and shape of the counterbalances.

- Hand to hand (see figure 10.7a)
- Shoulder to shoulder
- Back to back
- Side to side
- One is on knees: hands to back or front
- On shoulders: feet to feet (see figure 10.7b)
- One is lying down: feet to back or front (see figure 10.7c)

Figure 10.7 Counterbalances can be done by pushing to connect different parts of the body: *(a)* hand to hand; *(b)* feet to feet in a shoulder stand; *(c)* one lying, feet to back.

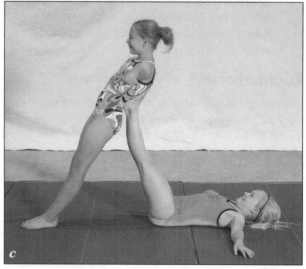

Early Attempts

Pupils' early attempts at counterbalances often result in the following:

- Overbalancing caused by unequal forces being applied
- Pyramid shape not clearly defined (base is too narrow)

 In the Pictorial Resources folder, refer to the Counterbalance file in the Partner Work folder.

Countertension

The paired balances shown in this section are not the only skills possible, and you should encourage your pupils to explore more variations. First experiment with the action of pulling by instructing pupils in the following Front Facing, Pull to Stand (Pulling) activity:

- Select a partner of a similar size.
- Sit on the floor facing each other with your knees bent and toes touching (tuck shape on buttocks).
- Attain the wrist grip.
- Pull on each other so that the arms are straight and both partners are leaning backwards.
- Maintain the pulling force and help each other to stand up, forming a V-shape.
- Keep the arms straight and the wrist grip firm.
- Reverse the process and return to the sitting position.

Entry, Execution and Exit Guidelines

- Partners position themselves close together with the body parts that will form the base of the V *almost* touching.
- Control, focus, tight: This is the formula for the safe performance of all balance skills.
- Partners adopt the wrist grip.
- Pulling on hands very slowly with control, the partners lean apart by straightening their arms to form a V-shape.
- Balance is held for 3 seconds.
- Partners return from the balance by pulling each other back to an upright position.

Ask pupils if they can countertension with their partner by exploring the following change mechanisms. This will alter the appearance and shape of countertensions (see figure 10.8).

- Change in height or level
- Change in direction

Figure 10.8 Various countertensions (pulling) may include *(a)* facing upright; *(b)* facing, one upright and one seated; or *(c)* kneeling showing change in level.

Early Attempts

Pupils' early attempts at countertensions often result in the following:

- Overbalancing caused by unequal forces being applied
- Incorrect wrist grip
- V-shape not clearly defined (base is too wide)

 In the Pictorial Resources folder, refer to the Countertension file in the Partner Work folder.

CHAPTER

Themed Games 11

The themed games in this chapter are variations of activities already used in most physical education lessons and may be familiar to teachers and pupils. These themed games are specific to gymnastics and relate to the unit of work being delivered, which is noted at the end of the description of each game.

Whilst the themed games have been used in the scheme of work on the DVD in the foundation stage and key stage 1 units of work only, they work equally well with key stage 2 pupils, who often request to play a specific themed game they enjoyed in a younger year group. If you can provide extensions and link additional ideas, the themed games will continue to provide some fun repetition and learning for older pupils.

Following is a brief description of each game in this chapter:

- **Space Finding Numbers:** This game uses and rehearses simple numeracy skills so that pupils understand the concepts of space.
- **Gymnastics Beans:** This game uses the idea of mimicking the shapes of various beans in interpreting basic gymnastics shapes and simple actions.
- **Road Traffic Signs:** Most children are familiar with travelling in a car and the associated road signals used in directing traffic and the unexpected obstacles that occur. Using road traffic tools, this game introduces basic gymnastics shapes and involves changing the direction and tempo of movement.
- **Washing the Clothes:** Most children are familiar with the functions of a washing machine. Using the washing of various articles of clothing, this game introduces all the basic and postural shapes in a fun and active way.
- **Creature Movements:** This game is a funny and creative means of encouraging various movement patterns based on the techniques animals use in travelling.
- **Physical Literacy Ideas:** These fun challenges are suitable for all age groups and ideal for use in the pulse raiser and mental preparation sections of the warm-up.

 Before beginning each lesson, obtain the Pictorial Resource cards for the specific themed games from the Themed Games folder on the bound-in DVD.

SPACE FINDING NUMBERS

This game is simple to instruct, enabling most pupils to understand the rules. The game identifies the properties of space and encourages an awareness of others and the use of teamwork, enabling safe movement in a physically active environment. Personal space is the area within immediate reach to a child's own body. General space is the area outside the immediate reach to a child's own body and is discovered through exploring the environment. Pupils find out how to control their own personal space in a general space setting when moving in an environment occupied by others and obstacles. When children move, they gain knowledge about their own bodies. This knowledge is referred to as body awareness and enables children to identify the location of and the use of their own body parts in functional movement activities. The development of body awareness contributes to the learning of spatial awareness, which is the ability to control the body whilst it is in motion.

Learning Intention

Understand personal space and general space.

Learning Outcome

Identify the properties of space and actively move into a space when necessary, displaying an awareness of others.

Pre-Game Activities

The pre-game activities include establishing a space and adopting the listening pose.

Establishing a Space

Identify the properties of a space. Pupils cannot be close enough to touch any other person or object.

Space finding strategies include placing non-slip markers on the floor and asking the pupils to spread their arms and turn around once slowly to see whether they are in space.

Adopting the Listening Pose

Identify the listening pose (ready position), which is any position where the child is still and looking at the teacher with hands clasped still in front of the body.

Scheme of Work

In the Pictorial Resources folder, refer to the Space Finding Numbers folder in the Themed Games folder. The Space Finding Numbers game is featured in unit 1 (Space, Listening Pose, Movement Patterns and Basic Shapes) in the scheme of work on the DVD.

How to Play

1. Ask the pupils to move carefully and quietly around the hall, ensuring that they can see and hear you at all times.

2. On an established signal, stop the pupils from moving and hold up one of the numbered cards (see figure 11.1). It is best to start with the number 1 card to assist pupils' understanding of space.

3. Pupils should adopt the listening pose when they have found their space.

4. When the class understands finding a space as individuals, you can introduce the higher-numbered cards (2, 3 and 4), which ask pupils to find a space in pairs or groups of three and four.

5. Where possible, do not use verbal instruction. Instead, use the visual guides to instruct pupils. This will ensure that all pupils are engaged and a peaceful controlled environment is maintained.

Game Variations and Extensions

With a key stage 1 or key stage 2 class, it is possible to extend the game with the following variations:

- Combine the game with the Travel Techniques resource card to vary the modes of travel.
- Ask pupils to form groups of more than four people.
- Ask pupils to form groups based on simple numeracy tasks (for example, 4 + 2, or 5 − 3, or 2 × 4, or 10 ÷ 5), and encourage pupils to solve the problem.
- Ask pupils to move around the hall using hand apparatus to do activities, such as the following:
  - Balance a beanbag on the head and pass a beanbag around the body.
  - Skip with a hoop and crawl through a hoop.
  - Roll a ball (*do not* allow pupils to lose contact with ball) and pass a ball around the body.

In the Pictorial Resources folder, refer to the Travel Techniques file in the Flight and Travel folder to share the modes of travel with your pupils.

☆ Teaching Points

Share the following teaching points with your pupils:

- When moving, look for the empty spaces.
- When moving, look where you are going.
- When moving, move with control, not too fast!

Figure 11.1 These numbered cards are full size on the DVD.

- On stop, make sure you (or your partner or your small group) are in a space.
- On stop, are you still? Don't fidget.

GYMNASTICS BEANS

This is a popular game to play with young children and can be used as an activity in a lesson (for example, in year R Space, Listening Pose, Movement Patterns and Basic Shapes) or as a tool to add variety to the warm-up. It can be used as a pulse raiser at the beginning of a lesson and helps to reinforce the basic shapes and actions that form the basis of the gymnastics formula (shape + action = gymnastics skill) used throughout the scheme of work in this resource.

Learning Intention

Learn three basic gymnastics shapes.

Learning Outcome

Respond to verbal instructions regarding performing the stretch shape, tuck shape and star shape.

Pre-Game Activity

The pre-game activity involves identifying shapes and actions and interpreting their meaning within the rules of the game. Pupils' must be familiar with three basic gymnastics shapes and four actions.

Here are the three basic gymnastics shapes that pupils' must be familiar with:

- Stretch shape is a string bean (see figure 11.2a).
- Tuck shape is a baked bean (see figure 11.2b).
- Star shape is a broad bean (see figure 11.2c).

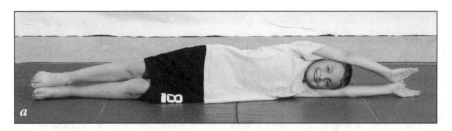

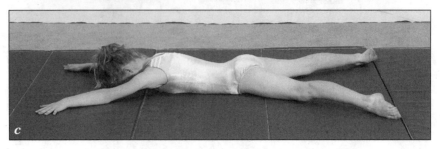

Figure 11.2 *(a)* The stretch shape is associated with a string bean. *(b)* The tuck shape is associated with a baked bean. *(c)* The star shape is associated with a broad bean.

Following are the actions used:

- Running is a runner bean (see figure 11.3*a*).
- Jumping is a jumping bean (see figure 11.3*b*).
- Wobbling (encouraging controlled wavy body movements similar to jellyfish) is a jelly bean (see figure 11.3*c*).
- Balancing is a frozen bean (see figure 11.3*d*).

a *b* *c*

d

Figure 11.3 *(a)* A running action is associated with a runner bean. *(b)* A jumping action is associated with a jumping bean. *(c)* A controlled wobbling action (similar to a jellyfish) is associated with a jelly bean. *(d)* A balance action is associated with a frozen bean.

Scheme of Work

 In the Pictorial Resources folder, refer to the Gymnastics Beans files in the Themed Games folder. The Gymnastics Beans game isfeatured in unit 1 (Space, Listening Pose, Movement Patterns and Basic Shapes) in the scheme of work on the DVD.

How to Play

1. Ask pupils to quietly find a space.
2. Ensure that pupils are familiar with the basic gymnastics shapes and actions.
3. Using the Gymnastics Bean cards from the DVD, instruct pupils on travelling and moving. To begin, pupils should remain in their own spaces to perform the following actions.
   - Runner bean: running (on the spot)
   - Jumping bean: jumping (on the spot)
   - Jelly bean: wobbly, wavy body movement
   - Frozen bean: balanced

4. When pupils achieve awareness of personal space, it will then be possible to ask them to move carefully and quietly around the hall to develop their awareness of general space. Ensure that they can see and hear you at all times.

Stop pupils performing the chosen action (running, jumping, wavy body movement, balance) by introducing the Gymnastics Bean cards representing the basic gymnastics shapes, which add gymnastics-specific skills to the game.

- String bean: stretch shape
- Baked bean: tuck shape
- Broad bean: star shape

5. Where possible, *do not* use verbal instruction. Instead, use visual guides to instruct pupils. This will ensure that all pupils are engaged and a peaceful and controlled environment is maintained.

Game Variations and Extensions

With a key stage 1 or key stage 2 class it is possible to extend the game with the following variations:

- Introduce a piece of hand apparatus to feature in the shapes.
- Perform shapes with a partner as a mirror image.
- Perform locomotor actions in a different direction. For example, run or jump sideways or backwards. Remember to instruct pupils to look in the direction of travel.

 ## Teaching Points

Share the following teaching points with your pupils:

- When moving, look for the empty spaces.
- When moving, look where you are going.
- When moving, move with control, not too fast!
- On stop, make sure you are in a space.
- On stop and in a shape, are you still? Don't fidget.
- Think about your shape:
    - Are you long and narrow for your stretch?
    - Are you compact for your tuck?
    - Are you flat and wide for your star?
- In your shape, point your toes.
- On performing the frozen bean balance, are you frozen and still?

ROAD TRAFFIC SIGNS

This is a fun game to introduce to young children to add variation to the warm-up. It can be used as a pulse raiser at the beginning of the lesson. Travelling in a car is a concept that most young children are familiar with.

Learning Intention

Reinforce basic gymnastics shapes using different parts of the body.

Learning Outcome

Demonstrate basic gymnastics shapes confidently.

Pre-Game Activity

The pre-game activity is identifying the shapes and interpreting their meaning within the rules of the game. Pupils need to be familiar with three basic gymnastics shapes and their associated road traffic ideas.

Following are the associated gymnastics shapes:

- Stretch shape is a pedestrian crossing (see figure 11.4a).
- Tuck shape is a traffic jam (see figure 11.4b).
- Star shape is a wide load (see figure 11.4c).

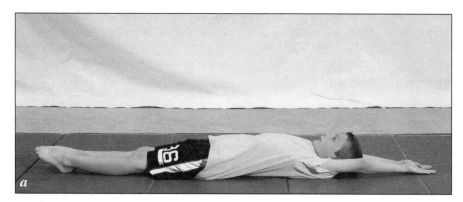

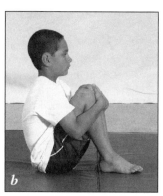

Figure 11.4 (a) Stretch shape is a pedestrian crossing. (b) Tuck shape is a traffic jam. (c) Star shape is a wide load.

Pupils should also understand the concept of the colours of traffic lights (red, amber and green):

- Red: Stop and be still.
- Amber: Jog on the spot.
- Green: Jog around the hall, moving in and out of the available spaces.

Scheme of Work

 In the Pictorial Resources folder, refer to the Road Traffic Signs files in the Themed Games folder. The Road Traffic Signs game is featured in unit 4 (Early Rolling Techniques and Climbing) on the DVD.

How to Play

1. Ensure that pupils are familiar with the road traffic signs and their associated basic gymnastics shapes.

2. Use the Traffic Lights cards (red, amber, green) from the DVD to instruct pupils on travelling and stopping.

3. When pupils move carefully and quietly around the hall, ensure that they can see and hear you at all times.

4. Use the Road Traffic Signs cards from the DVD (pedestrian crossing, traffic jam, wide load) to introduce obstacles to the game in the form of gymnastics-specific shapes.

5. Where possible, *do not* use verbal instruction. Instead, use visual guides to instruct pupils. This will ensure that all pupils are engaged and a peaceful and controlled environment is maintained.

Game Variations and Extensions

In key stage 1 and key stage 2 using varying speeds of travel and additional road traffic obstacles, you can extend the game and make it more interesting and challenging with the following variations:

- Use the gears of a car to change the speed of travel and direction of travel.
  - First gear: jogging
  - Second gear: skipping
  - Third gear: jogging feet to buttocks
  - Reverse: stopping and walking backwards, looking over the shoulder
- Use road traffic obstacles to change the travelling activity:
  - Roundabout: Get into groups of four or five (see figure 11.5) and, in a controlled manner, side step in a circle.
  - Speed bumps: Jump up and down.
  - Pick up a passenger: Link with a partner, hold hands and skip together. Pick up as many as four passengers.

Figure 11.5 Pupils gather in a circle to form a roundabout in the Road Traffic Signs game.

- Use further road traffic signs and ideas to introduce the two remaining basic gymnastics shapes:
  - Pike shape is a road block (see figure 11.6a).
  - Straddle shape sitting back to back with a partner is a car overtaking (see figure 11.6b).

Figure 11.6 *(a)* A pike shape is a road block. *(b)* A straddle shape sitting back to back represents a car overtaking.

Teaching Points

Share the following teaching points with your pupils:

- When moving, look for the empty spaces.
- When moving, look where you are going.
- When moving, move with control, not too fast!
- On stop, make sure you (or your partner or your small group) are in a space.
- On stop and in a shape, are you still? Don't fidget.
- Think about your shape:
  - Are you long and narrow for your stretch?
  - Are you compact for your tuck?
  - Are you flat and wide for your star?
  - Are you sitting up straight with straight legs and pointed toes for your straddle?
  - Are you demonstrating a right angle at your hips and have straight legs for your pike?
- In your shape, point your toes.
- When performing the roundabout activity, move with control, not too fast; hold hands firmly.

WASHING THE CLOTHES

This is a fun game to introduce to young children to add variation to the warm-up. It can be used as a pulse raiser at the beginning of the lesson. Washing clothes is a concept most young children are familiar with.

Learning Intention

Introduce pupils to postural shapes.

Learning Outcome

Demonstrate the box, front support and back support shapes.

Pre-Game Activity

The pre-game activity is identifying the shapes and interpreting their meaning within the rules of the game. Pupils must be familiar with the basic gymnastics shapes, gymnastics postural shapes and concepts relating to washing clothes.

Following are the associated basic gymnastics shapes:

- Tuck shape is a pair of shorts (see figure 11.7a).
- Star shape is a T-shirt (see figure 11.7b).
- Straddle shape is a dress (see figure 11.7c).
- Pike shape is a pair of trousers (see figure 11.7d).
- Stretch shape is a clothes line (see figure 11.7e).

Figure 11.7 *(a)* A tuck shape is a pair of shorts. *(b)* A star shape is a T-shirt. *(c)* A straddle shape is a dress. *(d)* A pike shape is a pair of trousers. *(e)* A stretch shape is a clothes line.

Following are the associated gymnastics postural shapes:

- Box shape is a washing machine (see figure 11.8*a*).
- Back support is a clothes peg (see figure 11.8*b*).
- Front support is an ironing board (see figure 11.8*c*).

Scheme of Work

In the Pictorial Resources folder, refer to the Washing the Clothes files in the Themed Games folder. Washing the Clothes is featured in unit 6 (Basic Shapes, Additional Rolling Techniques and Climbing) on the DVD.

How to Play

1. Ensure that pupils are familiar with the chosen articles of clothing and other items associated with the process of washing clothes.

2. Ensure that pupils are familiar with the basic and postural shapes associated with the named articles of clothing and washing items.

3. Ask pupils to move carefully and quietly around the hall, ensuring that they can see and hear you at all times. They should enact a story that follows a similar narrative: "The children have been outside playing in the mud and are very dirty. Their clothes need to be collected for the washing machine (box). First of all, gather the shorts (tuck shape). Continue walking and collect the dresses (straddle shape). Continue walking and find all the trousers (pike shape). Finally, put the T-shirts (star shape) in the washing basket. Place the clothes in the washing machine (box); after washing them, carry them out to the washing line (stretch shape). Hang the clothes on the line with the clothes pegs (back support). After the clothes blow in the breeze, it is time to collect the clothes. Carry the clothes inside and place them on the ironing board (front support) to be ironed."

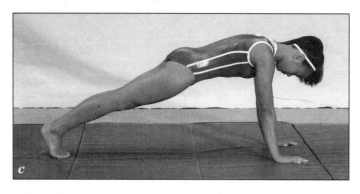

Figure 11.8   *(a)* A box shape is a washing machine. *(b)* A back support is a clothes peg. *(c)* A front support is an ironing board.

Game Variations and Extensions

You can extend the game with the following variations:

- Include some play activities that can be used as actions in a pulse raiser to start the game.
  - Sports: football (kicking a ball), tennis (hitting a ball with a racquet), netball (running and throwing and catching a ball), swimming (doing the best stroke or front crawl), climbing (pretending to climb upwards), skiing (slaloming).
  - Gardening: digging the soil, chopping wood, mowing the grass, sweeping up leaves, carrying heavy sacks of leaves or grass.
- Pupils could give themselves a scrub and a wash: Start at the top of the body (the face) and finish at the bottom of the body (the feet).
- The washing machine could go through a wash cycle involving some cyclic actions. For example, simulate washing actions or simulate spinning actions.

- The ironing of the clothes could be extended to encourage further development of core stability.
- Ask a pupil to tell a story for others to enact the actions that would link as a cross-curricular activity with literacy.

 Teaching Points

Share the following teaching points with your pupils:

- When moving to collect the washing, remember to walk in and out of the spaces.
- On stop and in a shape, make sure you are in a space.
- On stop and in a shape, are you still? Don't fidget.
- Think about your shape:
    - Are you long and narrow for your stretch?
    - Are you small and compact for your tuck?
    - Are you flat and wide for your star?
- Sit up straight with straight legs and pointed toes for your straddle.
- Sit up straight with straight legs for your pike.
- Make a square box shape for your box.
- Be strong in your middle for your front support.
- Push your tummy upwards for your back support.
- In your shape, point your toes.

CREATURE MOVEMENTS

Creature Movements is an excellent and fun game that introduces various means of travelling. It encourages a variety of movement patterns and uses various parts of the body to promote the fundamental categories of body management and locomotor skills. This playful themed game enables both young and older pupils to relate to the chosen animals and use their imagination to interpret the movement patterns. The varied movement patterns increase body awareness and aid knowledge and use of different body parts to develop the fundamental skills of balance, coordination and agility.

The themed game Creature Movements can be cross-curricular to promote the development of language (*slide, jump, stomp, gallop*) and as a numeracy aid by using shapes as a guideline to moving in the space available (*circle, square, triangle*). This game can be used as a tool for introducing and encouraging basic sequencing techniques in young pupils by joining together two or more different animal movement patterns.

Creature Movements can also be used as a challenging pulse raising activity in the warm-up. You can instruct more mature pupils either to vary the pace of the activity (slow, medium and fast) or to change the direction of travel (forwards, backwards and sideways). Once the pupils have learnt the movement patterns on the floor, you can incorporate hand apparatus to add variety and to make the activity more challenging to improve object control skills.

Learning Intention

Explore various ways to move and travel.

Learning Outcome

Physically demonstrate and verbally describe various movement patterns.

Creature Movements and Associated Animals

The chosen animals vary greatly in the way they move and are recognised by the distinct movement patterns they portray. Some movements are more complex than others. Following is an outline of each animal and its movement pattern in ascending order of difficulty:

1. Easiest
2. Challenging

3. Difficult

4. Most difficult

Easiest

- **Swooping bird:** Birds fly through the air, swooping up and down. Pupils should imitate a bird flying by moving around with their arms spread wide and changing their levels (see figure 11.9a-c).

- **Sliding snake:** Snakes slide and slither smoothly along the floor. Pupils should imitate the snake by sliding on large parts of the body (belly, side, back) along the floor by pushing and pulling with the hands and feet (see figure 11.9d).

- **Stomping elephant:** Elephants walk by stomping the feet and swinging the trunk. Pupils should imitate the walk by stomping their feet and swinging one arm in front of the body (see figure 11.9e).

- **Leaping frog:** Frogs move by jumping in an upwards and forwards motion. Pupils should imitate the frog by crouching down and jumping upwards to full stretch before finishing in a crouch (see figure 11.9f-g).

Figure 11.9 Easiest creature movements: *(a-c)* swooping bird; *(d)* sliding snake; *(e)* stomping elephant; *(f-g)* leaping frog.

Challenging

- **Galloping horse:** Horses gallop by lifting their feet in an upwards and forwards circular motion. Pupils should imitate the gallop by first lifting up the preferred knee and moving the foot in a circular motion to step forwards. They should step again immediately repeating the motion. (see figure 11.10*a-b*).

- **Scampering monkey:** Monkeys scamper along on their feet and hands. Pupils should imitate the monkey by running on their hands and feet with their buttocks upwards (see figure 11.10*c-d*).

- **Bouncing bunny:** Bunnies jump along, bouncing from their feet to their hands. Pupils should imitate the movement by transferring their weight from their feet to their hands whilst staying in a small, curled-up shape (see figure 11.10*e-f*).

- **Fluttering butterfly:** Butterflies flutter and float in the air, coming to rest on flowers. Pupils should imitate the action by moving around with their arms spread, waving them alternatively up and down, leaning from side to side and occasionally pausing (see figure 11.10*g-h*).

Figure 11.10 Challenging creature movements: *(a-b)* galloping horse; *(c-d)* scampering monkey; *(e-f)* bouncing bunny; *(g-h)* fluttering butterfly.

Difficult

- **Crawling caterpillar:** Caterpillars move by crawling along the ground in an undulating manner. Pupils should imitate the movement by folding in half on the hands and feet, walking their hands forwards until they are as stretched as is comfortable, then walking their feet back towards their hands (see figure 11.11*a-c*).
- **Creeping crocodile:** Crocodiles move by creeping along the ground. Pupils should imitate the walk by moving on their elbows and feet with their bellies near the floor (see figure 11.11*d-f*).
- **Lumbering bear:** Bears lumber slowly on their hands and feet. Pupils should imitate the walk by moving the right hand and right foot at the same time, then moving the left hand and left foot at the same time (see figure 11.11*g-h*).
- **Scurrying crab:** Crabs walk sideways on their hands and feet. Pupils should imitate the walk by travelling sideways on hands and feet with their belly to the ceiling (see figure 11.11*i*).

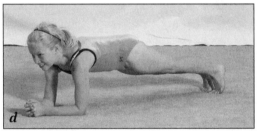

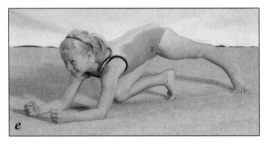

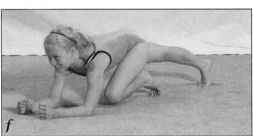

Figure 11.11 Difficult creature movements: *(a-c)* crawling caterpillar; *(d-f)* creeping crocodile; *(g-h)* lumbering bear; *(i)* scurrying crab.

Most Difficult

- **Running spider:** Spiders run around fast and slow, sometimes scaring people. Pupils should imitate the spider by moving on their hands and feet, swinging their legs and arms straight from side to side as they move (see figure 11.12*a-b*).
- **Swimming dolphin:** Dolphins swim elegantly by making waving movements with their bodies. Pupils should imitate the movements by stretching up tall and motioning their bodies in a wavy, curvy action (see figure 11.12*c-e*).

Figure 11.12 Most difficult creature movements: *(a-b)* running spider; *(c-e)* swimming dolphin.

☆ Teaching Points

Share the following teaching points with your pupils:

- When moving, look for the empty spaces.
- When moving, look where you are going.
- Think about the words that describe the way your animal moves: Are you moving like your chosen animal?

Scheme of Work

In the Pictorial Resources folder, refer to the Creature Movements files in the Themed Games folder. Creature Movements is featured in unit 7 (Jump, Land and Travel), unit 11 (Flighted Foot Patterns) and unit 15 (All Change).

Creature Movements can also be used as a whole unit of work with the following learning intentions and learning outcomes:

- Learning intention: Introduce the concept of sequencing.
- Learning outcome: Smoothly link various creature movements in composing a short sequence.
- Learning intention: Observe, copy and reflect on performances, considering various ways to enhance a performance.
- Learning outcome: Copy and learn another person's sequence and make positive contributions towards improvement of presentation.

The progressions in a Creature Movements unit of work could follow these guidelines:

- **Progression 1:** Acquire and develop the movement patterns associated with the Creature Movements cards.
- **Progression 2:** Select and apply the learnt movement patterns to compose short sequences.
- **Progression 3:** Show and teach your short sequence to a partner and in return learn your partner's short sequence.
- **Progression 4:** Evaluate and discuss techniques to improve performances of your own and others' short sequences.
- **Progression 5**: Include the use of hand apparatus to innovate and add variety to short sequences.
- **Progression 6:** Change the task by stipulating direction of the movement patterns, level of the movement patterns, and tempo of the movement patterns (these represent the ideas featured in unit 15 on the DVD).

PHYSICAL LITERACY IDEAS

As introduced in the preface and explained in chapter 1, physical literacy refers to the ability of interpreting and instructing the body to perform an action accurately and with confidence and recognizing the physical, social, cognitive and emotional attributes required for effective movement. Physical literacy ideas provide challenges for a pulse raiser in the warm-ups for a key stage 2 year group. The ideas are simple but challenging and good fun.

Learning Intention

Challenge the understanding of instructions regarding a physical task.

Learning Outcome

Translate verbal instructions into physical actions.

Pulse Raisers

The following physical literacy ideas can be used as pulse raisers:

- Place various body parts on the floor (such as hands on the floor).
- Place named body parts onto own named body parts (such as elbows onto knees).
- Join the same named body parts with a partner (such as hip to hip).
- Join together various named body parts with a partner (such as feet to knees).
- With a partner, perform a balanced shape with only the named body parts in contact with the floor (this is covered in unit 8 on the DVD and in chapter 1). An example is one back and two feet.
- Join with a partner to make a symmetrical shape or asymmetrical shape.

- Join with a partner in a gymnastics shape (such as stretch, star, tuck, pike, straddle).
- Join with a partner at a named body part in a named gymnastics shape (such as tuck shape, back to back).
- Create letters of the alphabet with the body.
- Join with a partner to form various letters of the alphabet.

The themed games and physical literacy ideas are fun activities to include in your gymnastics lessons. In all cases they are linked to the main focus of the gymnastics lesson.

Bibliography

Association for Physical Education. 2008. *Safe practice in physical education and school sport 2008.* Worcester, UK: Author.

Bailey, Richard. 2001. *Teaching physical education: A handbook for primary and secondary school teachers.* London: Routledge.

Bishop Sports and Leisure. *TOP gymnastics cards and handbook.* www.bishopsport.co.uk/product.asp?strParents=&CAT_ID=784&P_ID=6292.

British Heart Foundation. Jump rope for heart: Fun, fitness and fundraising (CD-ROM). www.bhf.org.uk.

Department for Education. 2010. Statutory framework for EYFS: Learning and development requirements. http://nationalstrategies.standards.dcsf.gov.uk/eyfs/site/requirements/learning/goals.htm.

Education Department of Western Australia. *Fundamental movement skills teacher resource.* www.steps-pd.co.uk.

Harris, J., and J. Elbourne. 1997. *Teaching health-related exercise at key stages 1 and 2.* Champaign, IL: Human Kinetics.

Hazeldine, R., and J. Cadman. 1984. *The body in action.* Leeds: National Coaching Foundation.

Macleod-Brudenell, Iain. 2004. *Advanced early years care & education: For levels 4 and 5.* Oxford: Heinemann.

Maude, Patricia. 2001. *Physical children, active teaching: Investigating physical literacy.* Buckingham: Open University Press.

Penny, Stephanie, Raywen Ford, Lawry Price, and Susan Young. 2002. *Teaching arts in primary school: Achieving QTS.* Exeter: Learning Matters.

Qualifications and Curriculum Development Agency [QCDA]. 2010. www.qcda.gov.uk.

Sabin, Val. *Primary school gymnastics for key stage 2.* Northampton, UK: Author. www.valsabinpublications.com/publications/gymnastics/key-stage-2.

Sabin, Val. *Primary school gymnastics for reception and key stage 1.* Northampton, UK: Author. www.valsabinpublications.com/publications/gymnastics/key-stage-1.

Tackle Sport Consultancy Limited. 2003. *Observing children moving: PEA UK 2003* (software package). Worcester, UK: Author.

Unit 2, module 4, The Beginnings of Behaviour, http://userwww.sfsu.edu/~psych200/unit2/24.htm.

Wilmore, J.H., and Costill, D.L. 1994. *Physiology of sport and exercise.* Champaign, IL: Human Kinetics.

About the Author

Lindsay Broomfield has been working alongside primary school teachers since 2003. As a youngster, Broomfield competed at national and international levels in artistic gymnastics. More recently, she has specialised in grassroots gymnastics through her own gymnastics club, developing children's basic elementary skills and fitness levels alongside gymnastics-specific skills.

Broomfield is a gymnastics tutor and has delivered Teachers Awards at primary and secondary levels. She has written teaching resources for UK Gymnastics and she tutors for the delivery agency in Wiltshire, delivering TOP Gym as part of the Primary Teachers' Continued Professional Development Programme. She is also qualified to tutor fundamentals and sports acrobatics.

Broomfield has been a part-time lecturer at the University of Winchester, delivering modules on physical development and physical education.

DVD-ROM User Instructions

System Requirements

Microsoft Windows

- PC compatible with Pentium processor
- Windows 2000/XP/Vista
- Adobe Reader 8.0
- Microsoft PowerPoint 2003 or higher
- 4x CD-ROM drive
- Dartviewer software

Accessing the Content

The PDFs on this DVD-ROM can only be accessed using a DVD-ROM drive in a computer (not a DVD player on a television). To access the PDFs, follow these instructions:

Microsoft Windows

1. Place the *Complete Guide to Primary Gymnastics DVD-ROM* in the DVD-ROM drive of your computer. (Note: The DVD-ROM must be present in the drive at all times.)
2. Double-click on the **My Computer** icon from your desktop.
3. Right-click on the DVD-ROM drive and select the **Open** option from the pop-up menu.
4. Open the file you wish to view. See the "Start00.pdf" file for a list of the contents.

Note: You must have Adobe Acrobat Reader to view the PDF files.

Your bound-in DVD includes detailed instruction and key coaching points for the major technical skills of primary gymnastics. By inserting the DVD-ROM into your DVD-ROM drive and running the **Dartviewer** software, you can study the key positions for each stage of the skill or even play a video clip when instructing your pupils.

Getting Started with Dartfish (Microsoft Windows only)

1. Insert the *Complete Guide to Primary Gymnastics DVD-ROM* into your computer's DVD-ROM drive. (Note: If your computer's auto-launch option is turned on, close the video player by clicking the X in the upper-right corner, then proceed to step 2.)
2. Select the **My Computer** icon from the desktop or Start menu.
3. Select the DVD-ROM drive.
4. Double-click the **Dartfish Mediabooks** folder.
5. If you already have the Dartviewer or Dartfish software installed on your computer, double-click any of the Dartfish files (**.dpa** files) in the Dartfish Mediabooks folder to begin. (Note: If you do not have the Dartfish software or have not yet installed the Dartviewer, follow the instructions below for installation.)

Installation Instructions for Dartviewer

1. Insert the *Complete Guide to Primary Gymnastics DVD-ROM* into your computer's DVD-ROM drive.
2. Select the **My Computer** icon from the desktop.
3. Select the DVD-ROM drive.
4. Double-click the **Dartfish Mediabooks** folder.
5. Double-click the **Dartviewer-install** icon and follow the instructions on the screen to complete installation.

Using Dartfish Content

Your *Complete Guide to Primary Gymnastics DVD-ROM* Dartfish mediabooks allow you to see video of the key positions of several different gymnastics technical skills. To use the mediabook in the Analysis View, first select the skill you'd like to view from the Analysis Selection list. Once you have chosen a skill, you can click the **Play** button to watch video of the entire skill. You can also click on any of the **Key Positions** for that skill at the bottom of the screen to read specific comments related to the proper execution of that key position. The Slideshow View of your mediabook allows you to see all the key positions of a particular skill and print those key positions along with their associated comments.